LIVE 8

HELLO WORLD

HELLO WORLD

Text by Paul Vallely

With captions by
Simon Trewin and Paul Gorman

Foreword by Bob Geldof

CENTURY

Paul Vallely is co-author of *Our Common Interest*,
the report of the Commission for Africa. As Africa
correspondent of The Times he covered the Ethiopian
famine of 1984/85 for which he was commended as
International Reporter of the Year. He then travelled
across Africa with Bob Geldof to decide how to spend
the money raised by Live Aid. He subsequently worked
with Bob Geldof on his best-selling autobiography,
Is That It? He has reported from 30 countries in the
developing world and was nominated for the UN Media
Peace Prize.

He has been chairman of the leading development
think-tank, the Catholic Institute for International Relations
(CIIR). He was also chairman of the fair trade organisation
Traidcraft. He has worked on special projects with the
development agencies Christian Aid and Cafod and has
been editorial adviser to the Catholic Bishops Conference
of England and Wales. He has written a number of books
including *Bad Samaritans: First World Ethics and Third
World Debt*. He is Associate Editor of The Independent.

Published by Century in 2005

1 3 5 7 9 10 8 6 4 2

Copyright © Woodcharm Ltd 2005
Foreword copyright © Bob Geldof 2005
Text copyright © Paul Vallely 2005

Design by Two Associates

Woodcharm Ltd has asserted its right under the Copyright,
Designs and Patents Act, 1988 to be identified as the
author of this work

First published in the United Kingdom in 2005 by Century
The Random House Group Limited
20 Vauxhall Bridge Road, London SW1V 2SA

Random House Australia (Pty) Limited
20 Alfred Street, Milsons Point, Sydney,
New South Wales 2061, Australia

Random House New Zealand Limited
18 Poland Road, Glenfield
Auckland 10, New Zealand

Random House South Africa (Pty) Limited
Endulini, 5a Jubilee Road, Parktown 2193, South Africa

The Random House Group Limited Reg. No. 954009
www.randomhouse.co.uk

A CIP catalogue record for this book is available
from the British Library

Papers used by Random House are natural, recyclable
products made from wood grown in sustainable forests.
The manufacturing processes conform to the
environmental regulations of the country of origin

ISBN 1 8460 50391
Printed and bound in Germany by Appl Druck, Wemding

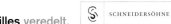

Foreword

Three days ago, in the late bright afternoon, I wandered across the scissor-mown lawns at Gleneagles. I found a little clearing among some trees and hunched down. Overhead the hummingbird helicopters clattered and thumped in the evening air as the world's most powerful people left what the Secretary General of the United Nations called the most successful and important G8 Summit for Africa there has ever been.

They couldn't see or hear me and I didn't really understand it, but I began to sob. I felt weird, empty. I don't know…It was over. It was over.

Because of this thing – this concert, event, lobby, protest, gathering, moment. Because of you. And the bands. And the crews and technicians and thousands of people who made this thing that was Live 8. Because of all this, the men in those helicopters had just written a cheque to double aid to $50 billion for the poor of Africa over the next few years. Unbelievable.

I thought, 'Now we have to make sure they cash it', and we will. We will get them to spend the money, we will name the corrupt who try and take one cent of it and we will speed up the 100 per cent debt cancellation for the poorest countries that was also confirmed at Gleneagles.

I think I cried because I was never sure it was going to work. That billions of us could force the men in charge to move. I was worried that they would remain for ever remote, unreachable in the isolated vacuum of their national power. But it did work. In the end there were just too many of us.

In other places in this book you will see what it was all about and what it means for the future of the poorest and weakest people on our world. You already know how we roared on behalf of those who were mute, how we moved power for the powerless, how we walked that long walk for many who cannot even crawl and how billions of us stood up for the beaten-down and put-upon.

We were led there by our bands, by musicians who articulate us better than we can ourselves. They talk a language understood by all humanity, and they have led us on this long twenty year journey from Live Aid. In their music is the sum of our longing for universal decency. They communicate dismay and disgust at the daily carnival of dying that parades across our TV screens. In the nightly pornography of poverty hundreds of thousands die annually simply because they are too poor to stay alive.

What a glorious, magnificent day. What a rejection of the defeat of cynicism, I thought as I watched the TV monitor side stage showing me four continents, nine countries and their greatest artists, nine cities and their greatest sites, millions physically present and thousands of millions spiritually there as we watched this one concert, one moment, one idea winding itself around what was truly one world that afternoon. And then I got a bizarre tickling sensation, thinking just maybe this is going to work.

Three days ago, crouched down among the chopper-beaten trees of Gleneagles I was shocked that 'the plan' had indeed worked. The Commission for Africa on which I worked was no longer just a theory for the reconstruction of a continent's economic life and, as a result, a better life for its inhabitants it was a paid-up reality.

The Long Walk. Over. The Summit. Over. The concert?

The concert plays out daily in my head. The magnificent bands. The brilliant young Turks and the ageless greats. I know them – they are not like what you read. They are not the mean-spirited midgets those tiny thorns of tabloid spite would have you believe. I know them as they appeared on that stage. They are great. And they are good.

As are you. At home. In the parks or streets or stadia or squares of the world on 2nd July 2005. This was the day we pulled it off. This was the day the powerful were powerless. When they bent in the force of our noisy gale. When we drowned out their endless No's by our boundless Yes. Where the promise of twenty years ago was realised. Everything that rock'n'roll had ever being about to me, or seemed to suggest or vaguely promised was made real on that beautiful day.

We should never need another event like it. But if we do, new generations know what must be done and they will not fail. The power of this wild music to call us to gather 'bout the electronic hearth of the TV or PC screen will continue. But will it, can it ever be expressed with such power, such elegance, passion and joy as on that summer's day last week?

My phone rang. I'd had it on 'loudspeaker' for weeks because it was constantly in use and I feared imminent brain cancer, ear rot, overheated temples or whatever.

Now with the helicopter noise I couldn't hear. I put it on 'normal' and tried to listen. I had to go. I wiped my eyes and stopped myself being shaky. Didn't want to look silly.

That's it for me, I thought, as I clambered into our minivan. On the ground the riot police and machine-gunned army waved us past the great security fences. Overhead the choppers thundered away across the glens carrying the men you had made listen.

I will never forget that day. Neither will you. Neither must you. Tell your children you were there. That you watched. That you changed the world. You and your mates. All 3.8 billion of them. And when they say why? tell them that you couldn't stand it. It wasn't fair. It wasn't right. A great injustice was being done. Tell them you were not powerless. Tell them that the bands played and you danced and sang and laughed and in so doing you allowed others you would never see or meet to do the same some day in the future.

We played our hearts out. 'And we played real good for free.'

Thanks for everything.

13/7/05
It _WAS_ 20 years ago today.
weird.

It was the moment when everything changed. It had been billed as the greatest rock show in the history of the world. Already the crowd in Hyde Park had seen on that one single stage Paul McCartney, U2, Coldplay, Elton John, Pete Doherty, Dido, the Stereophonics, REM, Ms Dynamite, Keane, Travis, Bob Geldof, Annie Lennox, UB40, Snoop Dogg and Razorlight.

And it was not even halfway through.

To come were Madonna, Snow Patrol, The Killers, Joss Stone, Scissor Sisters, Velvet Revolver, Sting, Mariah Carey, Robbie Williams, The Who, Pink Floyd and a finale with Paul McCartney again alongside George Michael and an all-star cast. And this was just one of ten Live 8 concerts taking place in a single day around the world, and bringing together a pantheon of the biggest names in pop music.

And more than that, the people in the crowds – and watching in their billions on television – knew why. At least in their heads they knew.

They had heard, over and over, that every day somewhere in the world 50,000 people die from illnesses that could easily be prevented – and of those 30,000 are in Africa. Every day. Every day. And for those whose minds had been numbed by the sheer weight of those terrible statistics someone had come up with a slogan, in an ironic echo of an advertising jingle, which said: 'Real people, really dying'. So the people had come. And they knew why. At least in their heads.

But then Bob Geldof, the organiser of this incredible assembly of musical talent, stepped onto the stage. 'Some of you were here twenty years ago, some of you were not even born. I want to show you why we started this long, long, long walk to justice,' he said. 'I want to show you, just in case you forgot, why we did this. Just watch this film.'

The giant screen behind him began to play a film from the Ethiopian famine of 1984/5. It showed African children crying, starving, staggering, waiting, dying. Images of stark, abject indignity followed one upon the other.

And then the film stopped on the face of a single child. Her eyes were closed by pain. Her parched lips were swollen with dehydration. The footage, cut surrealistically to a track by The Cars with the refrain 'Who's going to take you home?', had been shown at the original Live Aid concert. It had been the moment that stopped the world that day in 1985.

Twenty years on it did the same thing. The audience in Hyde Park stood stock-still. They were visibly shocked, their eyes wide with horror, their jaws dropped in with disbelief. Television cameras panned along the lines of a crowd in stunned silence.

Then Geldof spoke again. Those in the crowd who had been reading cynical newspaper stories about how aid to Africa was a waste of time might be wondering, he said, why we should even try to do anything.

'I'll tell you why? See this little girl? She had ten minutes to live twenty years ago. And because we did a concert in this city and in Philadelphia, and all of you came, and some of you weren't born, because we did that, last week she did her agricultural exams in the school she goes to in the northern Ethiopian highlands and she is here tonight. This little girl – Birhan. Don't let them tell us that this doesn't work . . . here is this beautiful woman.'

The crowd erupted in cheers and applause as onto the stage strode a striking young woman, beaming, with a smile that lit up the whole world.

There was about her the characteristic bearing of all the women of the Abyssinian highlands, noble, upright, confident, aristocratic. Her hair was plaited in cornrows across the crown of her head and then exploded in a glorious burst behind her. She wore a plain white dress, embroidered with blue Ethiopian crosses and covered in a shamma, a fine linen shawl. She looked like a princess.

It was a resurrection. The child had been snatched from the grasp of death and had become this fine young woman.

Suddenly everything was different for the crowds around the world at Live 8. They had been bludgeoned with facts, but they had not really understood. Now here was the person, Birhan Woldu, a 24-year-old woman who made flesh those statistics. Each one of the children who die needlessly somewhere – every three seconds – is a Birhan, brimming with possibility and potential, who could become confident, beautiful, intelligent, achieving and determined to make the world a better place. Here was the enormity of one life saved. Now do the multiplication.

Birhan, unfazed by the 200,000 people before her,

addressed the crowd. 'Hello from Africa. We Africans love you very much,' she said in her native Tigrinya. 'It is a great honour to be here to stand on the Live 8 stage. We love you very much. Thank you.'

Geldof then, moving 'from one immensely strong woman to another', introduced Madonna, the only person on the bill whose name and reputation had penetrated to Birhan's home village in the remote Ethiopian highlands. She had not heard of Paul McCartney or U2 or Elton John, but she knew about Madonna and had asked if she could speak to the world from the same stage as her.

It was a deeply emotional moment for both women. The pair hugged with an intensity not normally seen on a showbiz stage. The Queen of Pop, the ultimate professional, was momentarily overcome and swallowed hard to compose herself. She raised Birhan's hand in hers – two hands, black and white, in a gesture of equality and solidarity, held aloft – before launching into a powerful set.

Birhan's survival was a testament to the fact that aid – and the compassion that drives it – works, and that it works alongside the efforts of ordinary African people. Thanks to Live Aid and numerous other aid initiatives, countless Birhans have been saved.

Madonna continued to grasp Birhan's hand as she began her first song, 'Like a Prayer'. And beside the singer the young Ethiopian woman stood, like the answer to a prayer. She was a living reminder of what the world loses each time a child dies of starvation. And an implicit reprimand to those who refuse to act to prevent millions of lives being wiped away by poverty every year.

'Don't let them tell you that this stuff doesn't work,' Bob Geldof told the crowd. "It works – *you* work – very well indeed."

★ ★ ★

It was the concert Bob Geldof said would never take place. Over the past twenty years the Live Aid organiser has been inundated with requests by worthy causes. Each wanted his backing for some grand scheme or another. Many of them involved requests for another epic worldwide concert.

He has never even been tempted. 'It's a failure of imagination, they need to think of something new,' he

would say, whenever anyone proposed trying merely to replicate the 1985 global extravaganza. 'And anyway Son of Live Aid can never have the impact of the original.'

The world in which the original concert took place on 13 July 1985 was a very different place. That day the entire globe seemed to come together with a single common purpose and raised over $100 million, the most by far that had ever been collected for charity by a single event. In part, of course, its power came from emotion. The concert was a direct heartfelt response to the famine which killed not only Birhan's mother and sister but in which some 30 million people suffered as drought swept across sub-Saharan Africa.

Such terrible events had happened before. What was different about this one was the immediacy with which it reached the television screens of the affluent world. Children were dying before our very eyes, as we sat in our living rooms. A different level of reality broke through and shattered the complacency of our everyday lives.

On the day of the Live Aid concert the world stopped what it was doing to unite in a clear moment of absolute certainty. The largest audience ever seen – more than a billion and a half people, across the planet – joined together to do something unequivocally good.

Something changed inside those who watched the television that day – including two young men called Tony Blair and Gordon Brown who later went on to become the British Prime Minister and Chancellor of the Exchequer, in which jobs they made a massive step to change British policy towards Africa and placed the continent firmly on the agenda of the world's eight most powerful nations, the G8. Such was the emotional power of the collective experience that Gordon Brown said Live Aid was the single most important public event in the lives of two entire generations.

'We can never recapture that,' Geldof would moan softly as his aides repeatedly insisted that a critical moment had arrived in the history of modern Africa and that the time had come for another major international mass action.

But there was something else. It is hard now to comprehend what a technological feat the original concert had been. In 1985 there were no mobile phones and barely any fax machines. The laboriously punched ticker tape of the telex was the standard form of written international communication. In many countries international phone calls still had to be booked, sometimes hours in advance, through the operator. Computers were outside the experience of most ordinary people. The email was a future dream.

It had seemed a challenge bordering on the impossible to broadcast the first absolutely live, all-day, multi-artist concert to the whole world.

Yet simultaneous concerts on two continents were coordinated. Global television schedules were cleared. Concorde was put on stand-by. Even the Space Shuttle astronauts were lined up to make a contribution. That day 98 per cent of all the television screens in the world received the broadcast and viewers felt part of the biggest collective event in human history.

'How can we match that achievement in an era in which satellite broadcasting makes global communication a routine, easy, everyday experience,' said Geldof. 'In 1985 to see all the biggest bands in the world in one go was a unique event. Today you can see them all any day on MTV. Live Aid will be more powerful in memory than it ever could be in being repeated.'

Until only a matter of weeks ago Geldof was repeating this same line in private with his fellow campaigners. So what changed his mind?

★ ★ ★

The little helicopter swooped across the Thames taking Bob Geldof right into the heart of the concentric circles of security thrown up around London's Hyde Park on the morning of the Live 8 concert. And then the first thing he did was to march straight out of them. Before anything else, Geldof and his little entourage had to undertake a long walk not to justice but to Park Lane where the Live 8 organiser had undertaken to launch London's annual Gay Pride march.

It was not the most obvious way to kick off a day dedicated to raising awareness of the problems of Africa. But the gay community had booked Hyde Park for that day and then offered to hand the booking over to the Live 8 London concert. So Geldof wanted to say thank you.

'Shit, I've just had a horrible thought,' he said, in an uncharacteristic last-minute panic, as we made our way through columns of naked torsoed men towards the float where Sir Ian McKellen, Stephen Fry, Wayne Sleep

and other luminaries of the London gay scene were waiting. 'What if this lot aren't very keen on Africa because Africa's bishops are always saying terrible things about homosexuality?'

Try saying that one oppressed group will have an instinctive sympathy for another alienated people, even if they are the people of an entire continent, I suggested. Geldof climbed onto the lorry and he was off, elaborating about how rock'n'roll has always sung the song of the poor and the dispossessed, though not before some joshing about how secure he was in his masculinity. Even so, he had taken the precaution of removing the fetching pink cashmere jumper he had been wearing at home that morning before donning a round-collared white linen suit.

'Blair asked why I was wearing a Nehru suit. I told him it was supposed to be my white cotton Ghandi outfit,' he had told his partner, Jeanne Marine, as he was leaving home.

Actually Blair might have been right on the sartorial front (Gandhi more routinely wore a loincloth and shawl) but Geldof is right about the politics. One of Gandhi's slogans flashed up on the Live 8 screen later:
First they ignore you
Then they laugh at you
Then they fight you
Then you win.

As he left Park Lane to stride back to the Hyde Park stage, Geldof was constantly besieged by journalists intent on conducting on-the-hoof interview. He spoke to them, but without ever letting up on his relentless pace.

'Are you nervous?'
'No,' he replied, despite the fact that his entry in the visitors' book at Battersea Heliport an hour earlier had read: 'I'm nervous!'

'How big an audience are you hoping for?'
'There's a possible TV audience of five billion, though ultimately we're playing to an audience of just eight.'
'The eight leaders at the G8 in Gleneagles?'
'Exactly.'
'How will you measure success?'
'By whether they do what the Commission for Africa has asked for on aid, trade and debt.'
'Will today really make a difference?' asked a US journalist.
'It will be the greatest cultural event in the history of

the world. This will be a bigger broadcast than the Superbowl, the World Cup, even than the Olympics – and here nations won't compete, they will cooperate. All the promise of rock'n'roll is made concrete today. The answer is no longer blowing in the wind. There is nothing you can do that can't be done. All you do need is love.'

Geldof had been too busy that morning to listen to the radio. But ironically his technique of joining together song lyrics to make his point had been taken elevated to an art form by the novelist Rhidian Brook on BBC Radio 4's early-morning 'Thought for the Day' slot. Listeners had bombarded the station to get copies of the script:

Good morning, good morning, good morning,
London Calling, to the faraway town...
It was twenty years ago today,
And we've still got something to say
Not talking about London, Paris, New York, Munich.
Talking about my generation
There's a feeling I get when I look to the West.
And it makes me wonder.
Where is my beautiful car? Where is my beautiful house.
I want it now; I want it all. I want money.
Get back. I'm all right jack, keep your hands off my stack.
Money, it's a crime. Share it fairly but don't take a slice of my pie.
I read the news today, oh boy,
Mother, Mother, there's too many of you crying,
Brother, Brother, Brother there's far too many of you dying.
Help I need somebody
I'm just a poor boy nobody loves me...
Them belly full but them hungry.
You never give me your money, you only give me your funny paper...
Help me get my feet back on the ground - won't you please, please help me,
Don't leave me here all alone. Helpless. Helpless. Helpless.
Don't walk on by
Ticking away the moments that make up a dull day,
Fritter and waste the hours in an offhand way.

Cos, maybe you're gonna be the one that saves me.
There are still many rivers to cross and I still can't find my way over
Sometimes you can't make it on your own.
Don't give up, cos you have friends...
Imagine
Life is bigger; it's bigger than you
Consider this, the hint of the century
The world is full of refugees, a lot like you and a lot like me.
War is not the answer. You don't have to escalate.
Only love can conquer hate.
It's easy if you try.
Come on, everybody. Mr President. Come on. Come on. Let's go.
Jesus loves you more than you will know.
But it's a hard road to follow and a rough tough way to go.
What you going to do about it, what you going to do?
Nothing to do, it's up to you
You can't always get what you want,
But if you try sometimes, you get what you need.
Get up, stand up, stand up for your rights.
With or without you
Give a little bit. Give a little bit of my life for you.
While you see your chance, take it.
Are you such a dreamer, to put the world to rights.
Dry your eyes, mate. We can be heroes just for one day.
Today is gonna to be the day that they're gonna throw it back to you.
By now you should have found out, you realise what you gotta do.
Time to make the change, come on, you rock and rollers.
Look at the stars see how they shine for you
With the boys from the Mersey and the Thames and the Tyne...
All the people, so many people, and they all go hand in hand, hand in hand
Nothing to say but what a day
It's going to be a glorious day.
A beautiful day
I can feel it coming in the air tonight, O Lord...

Won't you help to sing these songs of freedom
Redemption songs?
Right here right now
You know we've got to find a way
To bring some loving here today.
And in the end the love you take is equal to the love
you make.

All the promises of rock'n'roll, made concrete in one day.

There was a flurry of interest as Geldof arrived in the artists' inner sanctum. Well-wishers surrounded him as he made his way through the compound of green cabins provided as dressing rooms in search of Bono. The well-wishers reached out, said hello or made lame jokes.

'Well done.'

'Thanks'.

'You're a genius, sir.'

'Thank you, dude.'

'By the way, Elton told me to tell you he's decided not to go on.'

'Great. Didn't want him anyway.'

Many were anxious to establish their credentials. One wore an original Live Aid shirt displaying all the signs of twenty years of laundretting. Another showed him his original Band Aid crew passes. 'Fucking hell,' said Bob, 'they must be worth something on ebay.'

The big screen in the artists' area was showing the Live 8 concert in Tokyo. A forest of arms were waving, fingers pointing, clutching sunflowers, and wearing the white wristbands of Hottokenai Sekai no Mazushisa, the Japanese equivalent of Make Poverty History.

Geldof glanced at it as he made his way to U2's cabin to talk to Bono and hear him try out his line: 'We don't want you to put your hand in your pocket. We want you to put your fist in the air.' Outside Elton John – who was only joking about not going on – was laughing with Coldplay's Chris Martin. Paul McCartney was sequestered in a glamorously decked-out mobile home. And Pete Townshend was making PG Tips in his motorised caravan.

Sting was sitting with a group of mates at a table outside his cabin. 'Apart from the importance of the cause,' he said, 'what is good about an occasion like this is getting to see other people. The way we work normally is that we are all isolated, like little princelings,

instead of having to share space with other people.' Even so, the hierarchy of pop was clearly in evidence, with a bouncer escorting Bono to the artists' gents, and standing outside, arms folded.

But if rock has its aristocracy they too can be overawed. 'This is amazing,' said U2 guitarist, The Edge, peering round at the firmament of stars, lost for words.

The UN Secretary General, Kofi Annan, walked in, and began a series of conversations with Bono, Geldof and Chris Martin. Geldof told the UN boss of a conversation he had recently had with Paul Wolfowitz, a close confidant of President George Bush and now President of the World Bank, the international community's premier development agency. His predecessor was Jim Wolfenson.

'Did you know the two names mean the same thing – son of the wolf?' Kofi Annan said.

'You obviously need lupine qualities for the job,' muttered Geldof. The World Bank is notorious among Make Poverty History campaigners for putting conditions onto its grants and loans to Africa which seem designed to benefit Western industry as much as African economies.

'We hope you will keep the pressure on after the G8 is over, and right up to the summit,' said the UN boss, referring to the UN summit in New York in September to discuss what the rich world can do to meet its commitments on the Millennium Development Goals to halve world poverty by 2015. To date the industrialised world has been all mouth and little money on the pledges.

'Of course,' said Geldof. 'Do you think the US will take the MDG summit seriously?'

These conversations filled the uneasy minutes as the clock ticked slowly towards the starting hour.

★ ★ ★

This time, like last, it had all begun again in Ethiopia. Now in January 2004 Bob Geldof was visiting friends. Someone told him that feeding camps had been set up again in the northern highlands, just as twenty years before during the great famine of 1984, and 1985. He drove north to see. It was not as bad as before, thank God, but the threat was that the scale of the food shortages could soon be worse even than in 1984, the year when Birhan had nearly died.

What filled Bob with something bordering on despair, however, were the reports on the news from the south of the country. He travelled there too – to the lush green fields of Kafe – the region from which coffee takes its name. In the past the people there would use the money they made from selling coffee to buy food. But the price of beans on world markets had crashed by almost seventy per cent after countries like Indonesia and Vietnam had dramatically increased coffee production. The farmers in the birthplace of the crop were earning so little that they could not afford to buy food. Famine set in. 'We call it globalisation,' Geldof said bitterly. 'They call it hunger.'

Geldof rang Tony Blair's office in Downing Street. They patched the call through to Evian in France, where the Prime Minister was attending a summit of the world's eight most powerful nations, the G8.

'It's happening again,' he exploded.

'Calm down,' said the Prime Minister, 'and tell me what the problem is.'

'I can't calm down,' said Geldof. 'Twenty years after Live Aid and things are no better. In some ways they're getting worse. What happened to all the early-warning systems we put in? What happened to the improvements in EU aid? None of it is working. And there are all these new forces of the globalised economy at play which nobody properly understands. Africa is fucked.'

'Come and see me when you get back,' said Blair.

Geldof did. What began to form in his mind was the notion that all the paradigms for development were outdated. They were based on the thinking of the Brandt report, which at the end of the 1970s – led by elder statesmen including the former German Chancellor Willy Brandt and the former British Prime Minister Edward Heath – had examined the relationship between the rich and poor worlds. The Brandt Commission's report 'North-South' had come up with the concept that 'enlightened self-interest' was needed if the North was to prevent an eventual violent explosion of discontent by the poor people of the global South.

But Brandt's analysis was out of date. It was a product of Cold War thinking. Since then the Berlin Wall had fallen. Apartheid had crumbled. September 11 had scarred the psyche of the Western world. Globalisation had accelerated and the world was no longer divided into power blocs. Instead, the tectonic faultlines were those of trade. A new Commission was needed. A political Band Aid, this time not run by politicians in retirement but by those in power.

Eventually, several meetings later, Tony Blair and his Chancellor, Gordon Brown, on whom Geldof worked separately, were persuaded. In February the Prime Minister announced a Commission for Africa made up of seventeen Commissioners, a majority of them African, from the worlds of government, business and the development sector. They included two prime ministers, a president and two finance ministers. To ensure the independence of the enterprise they invited Geldof to join too. They did not quite know what they were letting themselves in for. But nor did he.

Just before 2pm those involved in the opening trooped up the steep staircase to the stage. Geldof was stood at the top by a table on which were laid out dozens of microphones.

'Your cigars, gentlemen,' he announced.

'Ah Cuba – Cohiba,' said Bono, selecting the first.

The area at the side of the stage was a bizarre crush. Four French horn players, dressed like the Beatles from the cover of *Sgt Pepper*, mingled with U2 and Paul McCartney. In a more disciplined line at their side stood a dozen or so trumpeters of the Coldstream Guards, who won the prize – had there been one – for the day's most outrageous showbiz costumes, with their red tunics and hats of gleaming bearskin.

'There's a million already in Rome at the Circus Maximus,' Geldof told them. 'They're pouring into the Palace of Versailles. Tokyo is in full swing. Good luck.'

A medley from the original Live Aid in 1985 blares from the speakers at the 200,000 crowd before the huge stage – 'Rocking All Over The World', 'Don't Let The Sun Go Down On Me', 'Feed The World'.

McCartney, grim-faced, pursed his lips as the military trumpeters went past to blow the fanfare with which the event would start.

'Ten seconds,' someone shouted.

'Here we go,' said Macca, punching fists with each musician in turn.

At the control panel the red light went on for Mitch Johnson, the DJ known in the trade as 'the Voice of

'Hello, thanks for coming' – Bob Geldof

God' who was to be the Voice of Live 8. Beside him, looking nervous, sat a pasty-faced Richard Curtis, the writer of *Four Weddings and Funeral*, *Notting Hill* and *Love, Actually* and founder of Comic Relief and now, with his wife Emma Freud, a co-organiser of Live 8. He had given over the past year of his life to the Make Poverty History campaign and was there to supervise the concert's on-screen messages and between-act films. Beside him sat Lorna Dickinson, the exec producer for the BBC responsible for the worldwide broadcast.

'Ladies and gentlemen, it's two o'clock. This is Live 8, the greatest rock show in the history of the world,' boomed Mitch across the park, and the world. For once – as Paul McCartney and Bono, backed by the rest of U2, began to belt out 'It was twenty years ago today' – it did not sound like rock music's usual hyperbole.

In the park, stretched out before the huge stage, with a changeable electronic banner which read 'We'll be Watching You', 200,000 people went wild. They waved their own flags and banners in return. Flags of St George. Welsh dragons. Even a Red Hand of Ulster. Banners that said: 'Live 8 before it's 2 late', 'Hello world', 'Trade justice not free trade', and 'Wow Bob, it's huge'. Thousands more were gathered before large screens all around the country – in Manchester, Wrexham, Cardiff, Birmingham, Liverpool, Hull, Leeds, Gateshead, Bournemouth, Plymouth, Belfast, Inverness and the Channel Islands. At the other Live 8 concerts in Berlin, Johannesburg, Ontario, Moscow, Paris, Philadelphia, Rome, Tokyo and at the Eden Project in Cornwall there were almost three million people present. Across the world the television audience reached a peak of 3.8 billion people – more than half the population of the planet.

Someone said it was the first time that Paul McCartney had ever sung the title track from *Sgt Pepper's Lonely Hearts Club Band* in public. And if that was only one of many contributions to pop history that day it was no less poignant for that. Bob Geldof and, in truth, most watching sidestage had tears glistening in their eyes. Nor did the emotional temperature drop when McCartney pushed his way purposefully through the cram at the side of the stage and U2 took over. They released a cloud of two hundred white doves which peeled off across the stage as the band performed 'It's

a Beautiful Day' with lyrics adapted for the occasion.

'So this is our moment,' says Bono in declamatory mode. 'This is our time. This is our chance to stand up for what's right. We're not looking for charity. We're looking for justice.

'We can't fix every problem. But the ones we can fix, we must: 'three thousand Africans, mostly children, die every day of a mosquito bite. We can fix that.

'Nine thousand people dying every day of a preventable, treatable disease like Aids. We have got the drugs. We can help them.

'Dirty water, death by dirty water. Well, we can dig wells.'

So get up to the streets of Edinburgh, he told the crowd, and the band set the park rocking with 'Vertigo'.

'It's all downhill now!' laughed Geldof in the wings. 'Imagine having to go on after them,' he said to Midge Ure. 'Follow that!' So elated was he that he even hugged the ample figure of Harvey Goldsmith, who has grown to look more and more like a portly Edwardian gentleman in the years since Live Aid.

It had begun.

All around, the whirlwind blur was building. The stage revolved on a mighty turntable to bring the set-up for Coldplay to the front of the stage. Michael Stipe from REM rubbed shoulders with Sting in the three foot wide area which was to become – to Harvey's annoyance – a crowded celebrity spectator box. Kofi Annan sat on a platform perched above the speakers at the side with the artist Peter Blake, who had designed the covers for both *Sgt Pepper* and the original 1985 Live Aid programme, as well as that day's Live 8 one. Blake sat in his eyrie for ten full hours, drawing in pen in a small black sketch book until it got too dark to see.

Beneath all that, the elegantly wasted former Libertine, Pete Doherty, stood, his weight shifted to a single leg, with studied insouciance in a bumfreezer jacket and a bandsman's peaked cap. Excess being the watchword of youth, he wore both belt and braces. Roger Waters, soon to be publicly reunited with the rest of Pink Floyd after a not-speaking row that lasted more than twenty years, stood behind.

Geldof sauntered across and introduced Pete Doherty to his fourteen year-old daughter Pixie. 'She's in love with you,' he said, in the embarrassing way only a father can manage. Pixie seemed suddenly to find something very interesting to look at on the floor. She kept well out of sight the 'I love Pete' henna slogan on her wrist.

Just then, another Geldof daughter appeared. Peaches was sporting an ancient Boomtown Rats T-shirt which carried a picture of her dad in the days when he was about the same age as Pete Doherty. As Geldof introduced her to Doherty too, Pixie somehow found her voice and began to talk about Doherty's jacket. He got it at Top Shop but cut the label out because it was too embarrassing, he told her.

'He's got a great look. Very rock'n'roll,' said Geldof, quietly observing from a few yards back. Really, I said. 'Yes, but if you wore it you'd look like a prat,' he said with his usual complimentary turn of phrase. Doherty shambled towards us. He had found his disposable camera and was prepared to lower his cool for long enough to ask if he could have his photo taken with Bob.

Behind him Bill Gates, the founder of Microsoft and the world's richest man had made an appearance at the side of the stage. He wore a creamy yellow top with a blue sports shirt beneath. On his feet he wore plaited black leather loafers. He looked more out of place even than Kofi Annan in his tieless shirt and posh suit.

Gates grinned and began to read over the speech he was about to give, as racks of guitars on castors started to move on the revolve and Coldplay came off, having done 'Bitter Sweet Symphony' with the former Verve singer Richard Ashcroft. Chris Martin's parting shot as he left the stage and introduced a film about Africa was: 'It's probably the most important film you will see today. Just watch it. And if the BBC don't show it, they aren't doing their job properly.'

There was no screen by Bob Geldof on which he could check what the BBC did. In any case he was still musing on the song that had just ended. 'It takes incredible discipline to do a song like this in front of so many people,' he said, admiringly. 'You have to pull right back.'

At the back of the stage Tom Chaplin, the singer from Keane, was pacing up and down, looking as nervous as a sixth-former waiting to go into an exam. Roger Waters ambled by him and gave Geldof a big hug. 'Come on I'll introduce you to Bill Gates,' he said, facilitating another of the odd pairings of this oddest of days.

By the time Elton John went on stage – as only the fourth act – the show was ten minutes late the revised schedule which had estimated the London concert would end at 10.16 pm. That was already 45 minutes after the time the Royal Parks who owned the site wanted the final sounds to die away. Harvey began to get agitated.

Looking back on 1985 and Live Aid, its key characteristic was that it was about charity. It was good and noble but it had not sorted Africa's problems. It had addressed the symptoms and not the structures which were the root of the problem. It had asked: What can we do about Africa's poverty? It could not ask in those days of political deadlock: What keeps Africa so poor?

After Live Aid Geldof, Bono and others learned a swift lesson. Live Aid had raised around $100 million on the day, rising to almost double that with all the subsequent sales and merchandising. But they were shocked to learn soon afterwards that $100 million was merely the amount that African countries were obliged to pay back to rich countries in debt payments every three or four days.

Debt was a massive problem. The world's poorest countries have spent years paying off debts to the richest nations – instead of investing in their own people. For every $2 given in aid, at least $1 is spent by Africa on debt repayments. The Live Aid duo began to campaign for the cancellation of the debts.

They then learned about international trade. And how – through a complex web of rules, taxes, tariffs and quotas – the rich world takes far more from the poor than we give them. For every $1 we give in aid, we take $2 back through unfair trade.

We like to think we are generous to the poor, but the net flow of money is not from the rich world to the poor, but the other way round.

Next, they came to understand that the rich world does not merely refuse to help, but actually makes things worse. We impose trade tariffs which escalate if Africans try to process their own goods to make more money. The tax on raw materials like cocoa beans rises if they produce cocoa butter. It rises again if they add in sugar to turn it into chocolate. That explains why African countries which produce seventy per cent of the

world's cocoa make less than five per cent of the world's chocolate. We actually tax Africa's development.

And at the same time we in Europe, the United States and Japan subsidise our farmers to the tune of $350 billion a year a day – sixteen times what we give in aid to Africa. In recent years the average European cow has, grotesquely, earned more than the average African, receiving almost $2 a day in subsidies – double what many Africans earn. Japanese cows get $4 a day. It is the same story for sugar, cotton and much else. And a lot of this subsidised produce is exported to the Third World. Poor African farmers – unable to compete with these subsidised prices – go out of business. And their children starve.

When they are confronted by the bald truth of this the politicians of the rich world have promised – time and again – that things will change. But they do not. The report of Tony Blair's Commission for Africa contains a whole section headed 'Broken Promises'. It lists how pledges of aid are made, but not delivered. Targets for health or education are set, and ignored. Reform of farm subsidies, and an end to dumping produce in poor countries damaging their local farmers, are promised – and then subsidies are actually increased rather than cut. Changes in trade rules to help the poor are planned, then not delivered. People across Africa actually die as a result.

Five years ago, the world community made its greatest pledge. In 2000 in New York almost every world leader, and international body, signed up to a historic declaration. The Millennium Development Goals which ensued were an extraordinary plan which promised that by 2015 every child would be at school. That by 2015 avoidable infant deaths would be prevented. That by 2015 poverty would be halved.

At present rates of progress virtually every one of those solemn Millennium promises will be broken.

★ ★ ★

Bill Gates was reading and his lips were moving. He was learning his lines. Over his shoulder I see that his cue card had Dido's name written phonetically. Dye-do.

He was nervous. 'There's only five billion people watching,' he laughed. 'Though I guess that means that there could be half a billion who might like me even if I screw it up.' He paused, and added an afterthought. 'Maybe if I screw it up, they might like me more.'

Pause.

'There isn't an autocue is there?'

Elton John's final number, the T-Rex classic 'Children Of The Revolution' – performed as a duet with a Pete Doherty so laid-back that he threatened on occasion to fall over – ended. In the wings Sting clapped with his fingers splayed as wide as he could stretch them, making a curious flat sound.

Harvey Goldsmith was not in the mood for clapping anyone. 'I need more space,' he shouted. The schedule had slipped a little more and his irritation was turning to annoyance.

Geldof was unbothered. He sidled up to Lorna Dickinson at the BBC desk and said: 'Are you guys showing the rest of the world while the crew turn the bands around here?'

'It's only Tokyo and Berlin on air at present.'

'Who's playing in Germany?'

'No-one we'd want for the international feed. So we're just running interviews while the acts are changing round. When we've stockpiled enough stuff from the rest of the world we'll start running that.'

Brad Pitt was now in the wings too. 'Is there an autocue?' He obviously hadn't been talking to Bill Gates. It's down there, I told him.

'Is that it? Down there. It's tiny. Isn't there a big one out there?' he said, grinning boyishly and pointing towards the crowd in the hope that there would be one of those transparent prompter screens that politicians use so they can read their speeches and look, apparently, straight into the eyes of their audience.

'Nope. That's it.'

'Are you sure?'

'Come on,' said his make-up lady. 'I'll help you learn it.' And off they went.

The film which Chris Martin had been so insistent that the BBC show had not been seen by British TV viewers. The broadcasters had cut away from it – in favour of some celebrity interview with Jonathan Ross – for fear that showing it would be thought to compromise their political impartiality. Few of the between-act films made by the Make Poverty History campaign were seen by BBC viewers, but as the artists become aware that the BBC were not showing they devised a strategy.

Various singers began to beef up the introductions to their songs, knowing these could not be cut.

Dido addressed the G8 leaders directly: 'There are millions and millions of voices asking you to do the right thing and we will be waiting.'

'We as a nation have robbed, killed, tortured and stolen from the Third World for centuries,' said Ms Dynamite. 'If there is a debt to be paid then surely we are the ones that owe it,' she added as she launched into Bob Marley's 'Redemption Song'.

'All you need is love – John Lennon said that,' shouted Johnny Borrell of Razorlight. 'Music can change the world – Bono said that. Sign the fucking petition – I said that.'

Harvey was looking at the clock again. 'Bob,' he said, approaching Geldof. 'We're running twenty minutes behind now. You're not thinking of playing are you?' Geldof was not down on the running order. But Harvey had heard a rumour.

Geldof has learned from his contact with politicians that saying nothing is preferable to lying. He did not reply.

★ ★ ★

It seemed a funny place to stop. But Geldof was clear. 'Here,' he snapped. 'Pull over here.'

At the side of the road was a broad sweeping valley. It looked no different from a hundred others we had passed on our long journey through the Abyssinian highlands. We were only minutes away from one of Ethiopia's most antique cultural capitals, the little town of Lalibela, which is the site of a breathtaking series of underground churches hewn by hand from the rock of the ancient plateau. So why stop here?

Geldof got out of the car and walked over to the side of the road. 'This is the place,' he said, and then stared silently into the valley for what seemed like an age.

And then he explained. It was twenty years since he first came to this spot. The then Marxist government of Ethiopia had wanted to show the place off to him, partly because of its venerable history, but mainly because they had just taken it from the rebel army in what felt like an interminable civil war. It was 1985. The year of Live Aid.

'It's an impossibly beautiful place,' Bob began, 'When I first came this green landscape was naked brown soil.

The earth had been burned by the remorseless sun which had brought the drought and famine. It had cauterised this entire land. There were tanks and men with guns everywhere. It felt a menacing place, in many more ways than one.

'When we got to this valley it was dusk and I suddenly became aware of tiny pinpricks of light. They started over there,' he said, pointing, 'and then spread, gradually across the valley, and then up the hillside, and onto the top of the plateau. Like little fireflies illuminating themselves in a chain sequence across the whole landscape. Then someone told me what they were.'

They were fires. And they were being lit by desperate people who had abandoned their homes and trekked for days, and sometimes weeks, to a place where they heard there was food aid to be found. It was the story of countless families like that of Birhan. Some of them made it, but many did not.

When the sun fell, and this entire population on the move knew they could not reach their destination for the night. So they made camp where they were, drew their thick white woollen blankets around them against the bitter cold of the mountain night. Each, if they had found wood on the journey, lit a tiny fire.

'The hillside came alive with fires,' said Geldof with a curious steady detachment. 'But I knew what each one represented, because I had seen those scenes close-up elsewhere already. Parents giving the last of their food to their children – some of whom were so weakened that they would die that night. Children who had been left orphaned by the journey. Eight-year-olds carrying three-year-olds. An intolerable vision. Like a painting of hell.'

And then something so bizarre happened that you wouldn't believe it if someone put it in a novel.

'Just down there, to the right, there must have been an aid workers' camp, because I heard a radio. It was a long way off, but the sound carried. It was the BBC World Service. After a while it began to play the Band Aid single, 'Do They Know it's Christmas.' I was horrified, at the triteness of our response set against the immensity of this reality.

'And then, when it got to Bono's line, his voice rang out with utter clarity. And as he sang: 'Tonight, thank God it's them instead of you' I started to cry.'

When I turned from the empty landscape to look at Geldof he was crying again, twenty years on.

The eucalyptus trees were in flower as we entered Lalibela, a dusty little place of several hundred mud huts, some of them substantial and a few more than four hundred years old. But Lalibela's treasures were hidden from view. Hens clucked in the yards around the doors. Pigeons were cooing. Soft smoke rose gently from the roofs. The warm smell of bread wafted up from the houses lower down the hillside and mingled with the scent of meat cooking caught on the breeze as we moved through the town.

The place was about its normal business. A boy of six or seven walked past with a tin of cow manure on his head. Others carried sticks of sugar cane which they had bought with the small coins they had earned from showing tourists secret churches which become visible to the stranger only when you are literally a few feet away from them. A runaway bullock shouldered its way suddenly through the crowds and made off down the roadside track.

'Stop that cow,' shouted the hapless man who had just bought it at market and was chasing it – to the laughter, it seemed, of the entire town.

In the market there were great piles of grain, though much of it was dusty and some of it the worse for termite attacks. There was coffee, green, khaki and black. There was rock salt for people, and salt cakes for animals, brought by merchants hundreds of miles from the Djibouti coast. There were plastic bowls and basins, and trays of cheap watches. There were Muslim weavers selling their produce, alongside traders with colourful fabrics from China; globalisation has tentacles that reach into the remotest mountain fastnesses. There were children selling Jolly Juice, a concoction made from tinned orange powder and dodgy-looking water.

There was nothing to remind Geldof of the terrible days of 1984/5. Apart from the flies. One of the most haunting images for a Westerner arriving at the height of the famine was of children too weak to wipe the flies from their faces. But if you arrive today in the Ethiopian highlands at the wrong time of year the flies are there still, and in such numbers that you feel as though you are trapped inside a buzzing black cloud. Even the outsider eventually becomes too weary to ceaselessly swish the insistent insects from your face and arms.

May to September is the terrible time, until the frosts come to kill them off in October.

But the children seemed unfazed. They carried on happily, busy in their mercantilist enterprises, or happy at play with stones or sticks, hoops made from twisted circles of wire, or kicking a misshaped football.

'Isn't it great to see these kids looking so healthy,' said Geldof, ruffling the hair of a boy walking beside him who stared up at the gangly white man with undisguised curiosity. Twenty years ago he had avoided touching the children for fear a photographer would snap what he called a 'White St Bob nurses Sick Black Baby' picture. Things were different now. These children had smiles and chubby cheeks, and a sheen in their hair; they shouted and laughed, tripped up their mums and were shouted at.

A curly-haired boy, aged about twelve, in a Chicago Bulls T-shirt approached Geldof. 'I will be your guide,' he said, more in declaration than in request.

'Will you now,' said Geldof with a laugh; presumptuousness has, after all, been a classic Geldofian trademark from his early days as pushy post-punk to his more recent refusals to take No as an answer from prime ministers and presidents.

The boy's name was Chombe. By day, he said in remarkably good English, he guided tourists around the churches; by night he went to the monastery, which was the only place with electric light, so he could read. 'I want to be a doctor,' he said, 'or a pilot'.

Africa is everywhere a place of paradox. Geldof's trip across it threw up paradoxes aplenty, like the satellite dishes emerging from the thatched roofs of mud huts, the monument to Soviet MiG fighters now used to give shade to donkeys pulling water carts, or the beggar with deformities which would have looked medieval were it not for the two pairs of flip-flops he wore on his knees and hands. All these tell us things which are both expected and unexpected about the relationship between Africa and the supposed civilised world.

'Look at that,' Geldof pointed out in one backwoods market town. A boy had passed by wearing a T-shirt which bore the legend: I Am Not A Tourist. 'Postmodern or what?'

But some apparent paradoxes are really just our Western prejudices in disguise. Nowadays even the smallest and dustiest African village seems to have an internet café powered by a noisy old generator and a satellite phone.

'And why not?' said Geldof. 'We so often unthinkingly suppose that progress means moving from tradition to modernity. We see progress as about the rest of the world 'catching up' with the West. Yet part of the genius of Africa is its ability to take what it sees as good, but to hang on to what it sees as better.'

Nowhere was that more clear than in a hospital in Hargeisa in Somaliland. There are four 'normal' hospitals and this one. It was an unprepossessing place: tatty, unpainted, badly lit. But the doctor in charge there, Dr Hussein Adan, had been trained as both a traditional African healer and in Western medicine. By fusing the two he had developed a way of replacing shattered limbs with a technology that involved the implantation of camel bones into the legs of men and goat bones into the heads of children. It was all sterilised with a mixture of camel's milk and paste from the bark of desert shrubs – and then treated with antibiotics. Incredibly it works, even with brain surgery.

Geldof there met an eighteen year-old girl. Her head was crushed in a car crash. 'Her brain came out on the road,' the doctor explained. 'We brought her in, removed the stones and grit from her brain, and then used a mixture of frankincense and camel milk to clean it. Then we covered the hole in her head with a piece of goat bone.' The girl was sitting up in bed. 'She's not well but she's improving.'

Camel bones and goat bones, frankincense and antibiotics, and camel milk with everything. It sounds preposterous. But, like so much else in Africa, amazingly, it works. 'And the striking thing,' said Geldof, 'is that tradition and modernity are not opposites, or a starting and a finishing point. They are something which fuses to make a singular African solution'.

We saw that in politics too. Under the shade of an acacia thorn we came across a group of elders from one of the clans that traditionally govern Somalia. They were drinking camel milk from a communal cup. But it was not a social gathering. It was a meeting under an ancient and complex system known as the Tol, under which responsibility for crime lies not with an individual but with his clan.

It works like this. If a man steals a camel his clansmen will say: 'Where did you get that?' Social pressure

forces him to tell them, whereupon they reply: 'Well take it back, or else his clan will come to us and demand that we all pay compensation.' The system worked for centuries. But then as warlords took over control in post-colonial Somalia they abolished the Tol. Anarchy ensued. By contrast, in the breakaway area known as Somaliland, it has not only been retained but has been elevated to the status of the second chamber of parliament. Few there doubt that this is one of the key factors in the relative stability of Somaliland.

'This odd mix of African and Western systems of governance clearly works,' Bob said. 'The evidence on the ground is that tradition does not inevitably precede modernity. It is the interaction between the two that in Africa will bring change and progress. Yes, of course Africa is still plagued by drought, famine, hunger, disease, corruption, bad government and conflict. But things are not as the Afro-pessimists suggest.'

Instead there is a sense of flux, and of opportunity. 'There is dynamism in the air, and change,' Geldof reflected as we sat in a bar in Addis Ababa. It was true. Africa today is very different from the place we first visited twenty years ago at the time of Live Aid. In those days there were about twenty wars going on across the continent; today there are just four. Then half of all African countries were dictatorships; today more than two-thirds of the countries in sub-Saharan Africa have had free-ish and fair-ish multi-party elections. Some have even produced changes of government.

'Of course, creeps like Mugabe hang on in Zimbabwe which should be regarded as a rogue state as representative of Africa as North Korea is of Asia. But elsewhere a new generation of political leaders is emerging, many of whom show a commitment to the common good of the people. Almost half of all African countries had economic growth of more than five per cent in 2003. But over the past five or so years the signs are that change is beginning to sweep like a tide across the continent. 'There's the start of what could be a real momentum for change.'

We stayed up too late, and drank too much, on our last night in Lalibela. Just before dawn I staggered to the bathroom, glancing out of the uncurtained window on the way. What I saw made me bang on the wall to wake Bob in the room next door.

Out of the window was the other end of the same

valley we had encountered when we first arrived. A light flickered on the far hill. Then another and another, in an eerie echo of that desperate trek of twenty years before.

But this time the cause was different. It was the feast of Meskal.

As we looked out from our adjacent balconies the whole valley slowly lit up with individual families lighting fires and illuminating the insides of their homes with burning brands in blessing. Noises of rejoicing filled the air. Children shouted excitedly, provoking dogs to bark, donkeys to bray and cocks to crow before their time. As the pinpricks of light spread the valley filled with that most African sound of celebration as the women let rip a strange ululating sound from the back of their throats.

Bob Geldof watched and listened, this time his eyes aglow with joy. The fires of despair seemed to have given way to the flames of hope.

★ ★ ★

By mid-afternoon nerves were beginning to jangle backstage. Even seasoned performers were anxious at the scale of what they saw before them. Brad Pitt was squatting on his haunches and doing breathing exercises. Bill Gates was giving his cue cards such serious attention that they had gone all bendy.

Only Bob Geldof seemed immune. Keane's lead singer, Tom Chaplin, was pacing round in circles at the back of the stage as a variation, it seemed on his earlier back-and-forth caged tiger sort of movements. Geldof helpfully clapped him on the back at one point and said: 'Don't be nervous. There's only five thousand million people watching you.'

'Thanks, Bob.'

Just before 3.30 pm Geldof made his first appearance on the Live 8 stage. 'Look busy, it's the boss,' someone shouted. A huge roar of applause went up. 'Thanks for coming,' he told the crowd. 'It would have been a bit crap if no one had showed up.'

He proceeded to bring on someone few people in the worldwide audience could have been expecting. 'I want to introduce one of the men who invented the modern world and billions of people are watching us now because of him,' Geldof said. 'He is one of the great businessmen of our time and certainly the greatest philanthropist of our age. He says our plan is the right plan, it's the only plan. Ladies and gentleman, one of our biggest

supporters, Bill Gates.'

The crowd roared in a mixture of surprise and approval. Perhaps they knew that Gates and his wife Melinda have personally so far given $5 billion towards relieving poverty. The plan Geldof referred to was the comprehensive package of more than ninety recommendations made by the Commission for Africa, a good number of the more radical ones at Bob Geldof's direct instigation.

'I believe that if you show people the problems and you show them the solutions they will be moved to act,' Gates told the crowd.

'I have learned that success depends on knowing what works and bringing resources to the problem. We know what to do. The huge turnout for Live 8 here and around the world proves that. The generosity we are asking for can save millions of lives. Some day in the future all people no matter where they are born will be able to lead a healthy life.' The crowd roared their approval. 'We can do this and when we do it will be the best thing that humanity has ever done.' It won him from the 200,000 people in Hyde Park one of the biggest cheers of the day.

He ambled back to the side of the stage wearing a bashful grin.

But when he got there he found no one else was laughing. The schedule had slipped still further and Harvey Goldsmith – clearly worried that the Royal Parks might never allow him to do a show in their parks again – had moved up several gears from agitated through annoyed to rather angry.

Harvey was shouting at the Voice of God.

'Go!'

'Harvey, I'm waiting for a cue from the BBC,' said Mitch.

'Go!!'

Now he shouted at the Lorna from the BBC.

'I've lost all talkback,' she replied calmly, pressing buttons that ought to have got her through to the rest of the BBC operation in various places elsewhere on the huge site.

'Philadelphia is going live at 5pm,' she said to Harvey. 'Make sure that Keane is off by 5pm.'

The veins in Harvey's neck started to bulge. It was him who was trying to get people off, and everybody else who was buggering about wasting time, he would presumably have said. Had he not been rendered speechless at that point.

'Will Smith will be ready to go live at 5.'

'Stand by for voiceover.'

'Are you introducing Travis?' Harvey shouted at Mitch. 'Will someone tell me what the hell is going on! We're running late.'

Richard Curtis, sitting in the middle of it all, looked pale and drawn. He is a nice, polite, measured chap. He was clearly not used to this kind of carry-on. Curtis fiddled with the loose label from his water bottle as one of his slogans flashed up on the screen: 'Real people, really dying'.

'OK,' said Lorna, the BBC exec. 'The crowds in each country are, consecutively, going to say hello to each other. This is something that has never been done in broadcasting ever before. Rome, Paris, Berlin, Johannesburg, Ontario, London, Philadelphia. . . If there's going to be a bloomer it will be now. This is the global bloomer moment . . . '

'We're running late, I said,' bawled Harvey. 'We're running later and later.'

Lorna jabbed one of her buttons. 'London calling Philadelphia. . . And Philadelphia isn't answering.'

'One minute ten seconds to go,' shouted a technician.

'Sh. . . ugar,' said the polite lady from the BBC, almost from a Richard Curtis script.

'Will someone tell me what the fuck is going on?'

'We have to join the world. This is the moment. This is what it's all about, Harvey. You want an event that runs on time. But we want a global TV moment.'

'One minute to Philadelphia.'

'Oh God. There's no sound.'

Over in the United States the rap star and actor Will Smith began to speak. At least his lips were moving. Perhaps he was miming.

'There's no bloody sound!'

★ ★ ★

So what did Bob Geldof conclude at the end of a year with the Commission for Africa?

First, that things are starting to improve on that continent. After nearly forty years of stagnation many African countries are seeing the beginnings of democracy and real economic growth. Just maybe and fingers crossed this time it'll work.

But it also concludes that without the backing of the rich world these green shoots of recovery and reform would be burned up in the merciless African sun. Wealthy nations needed to do three things. First, they must double levels of aid to $50 billion a year. Second, they must wipe away one hundred per cent of the debts of the world's poorest countries. And third, they must reform world trade to end its bias against the poor.

One key factor, Geldof and his fellow Commissioners concluded, underlies almost all Africa's difficulties over the past forty years. It is poor government.

Good government, Geldof found, requires African governments to make themselves more open to the scrutiny of their citizens. That means strengthening parliaments, the media, trade unions and the judiciary. It means making budget processes more open so voters can see where money is being allocated, and ensure it is spent as promised. Aid is vital to all that.

Only that kind of scrutiny can, ultimately, stem the rot of corruption which is a problem found in Africa at all levels. But, as Geldof became fond of saying, it takes two to tango on corruption – someone to give the bribe and someone to take it. That means we in the rich world have a role to play. Western firms who bribe should be refused export credits. And our companies, especially those in the oil and mining industries, must be made to publish what they pay to African governments. Openness by firms will force openness by governments.

Rich nations can help in another way. They should track down money looted by corrupt African leaders, now sitting in foreign bank accounts. And they should send that money back to the people from whom it was stolen. This will send out a clear message to current and future leaders that they will not be allowed to profit from such immoral behaviour.

Another key area is in creating the right economic, social and legal conditions to encourage firms and individuals to invest. That means legal systems to protect basic property rights and respect for contracts. It means the rich world should double its aid for building infrastructure – from rural roads and small-scale irrigation to slum upgrading and larger projects including regional highways, railways, power plants and

information and communications technology.

Africa cannot grow without trade. Africa is confronted by trade barriers that tax its goods as they enter the markets of the rich world. Rich countries must dismantle these and other barmy rules. We must also axe the $350 billion a year we spend subsidising our farmers which allows cut-price exports from Europe and the US to drive African farmers out of work. And we must stop saying in world trade talks that concessions will only be made to Africa if Africa makes other concessions in return.

But contrary to what Bob Geldof expected at the outset, he found that trade barriers are not the prime cause of Africa's trading problems. China and India have faced even higher barriers and yet have still broken into world markets. The big problem is that Africa does not produce enough goods, of the right quality or price, to enable it to trade more internationally. Nor do African nations trade enough between themselves. A mere 12 per cent of all African goods go to other African countries.

To improve its ability to trade, Africa needs to improve transport and roads to make goods cheaper to move. It must scrap tariffs between one African country and another. It must abolish red tape and cumbersome customs procedures. It must make it easier to set up businesses. Many of these changes are easy, cheap, quick and in the hands of Africa itself. In Mozambique, goods are now cleared forty times faster than before customs reforms took place. More aid from rich nations can help fund all these changes.

The amounts involved are large – the equivalent of a Marshall Plan for Africa. But the costs to the rich world are relatively small. The first $25 billion increase that Live 8 called for – and got – represents just ten pence out of every £100 that the rich world earns.

There will be those who'll argue that this aid does not work. But the Commission has done an extensive study on aid and found it has improved significantly in recent years. The World Bank estimates that the average rate of return on its aid is now twenty per cent – better than you'd get in any building society. And the commission sets out a raft of proposals on how aid can be made better still.

There is one other thing. The problems Africa faces are interlocking. Poverty is a series of vicious circles that reinforce one another. They must, therefore, be tackled together. Unless there is a big push across a broad front Africa will not make the leap out of poverty and into prosperity.

That was the platform which Geldof and his fellows endorsed. But would the G8 back it?

★ ★ ★

It was 5pm. Bob Geldof returned to the stage to tell the Live 8 crowds in Hyde Park: 'There are three billion people watching you right this moment.' They roared in delight.

'I want to say hello to Paris and Rome and Berlin and Tokyo and Toronto and Johannesburg and right this second, in 84 degrees in Philadelphia, one million people are on the streets. Welcome, America, to Live 8. Here is Will Smith.'

Rome cheered Paris, Paris cheered Berlin, and on it went through the chain to Johannesburg, Ontario, London and Philadelphia. Eight cities, four continents, one moment, one concert, one people, one world.

It ended in the United States with the actor and rap artist, Will Smith. And the world could hear him as he spoke. The heart-stopping terrible silence had been a temporary fault in the BBC control desk. Lorna Dickinson clapped in relief as the sound was restored to her monitor.

Two heavies stood behind Will Smith. But they were not there to protect the movie actor. Behind him in a large frame was the American Declaration of Independence with him. 'I am honoured,' he said, 'to be here in my home town of Philadelphia, sharing the stage with this symbol of our nation's enduring commitment to the beautiful and profound idea that we are all created equally.'

But this weekend, as the American people prepared for their traditional fourth of July Independence celebrations, should, he said, mark a worldwide Declaration of Inter-dependence.

Smith celebrated this notion of international solidarity by wearing a T-shirt bearing the legend 46664 – the prison number of Nelson Mandela on Robben Island during his two decades of incarceration as South Africa struggled to liberate itself from apartheid. It was a struggle in which the ordinary peoples of the rest of the world had lent their support in whatever way they could.

As the live links built up around the world the Hollywood star brought the scale of the event into perspective: 'Right now you're watching millions of live spectators and maybe billions more tuning in around the world. So mark this moment.'

But then came a message that stilled the crowd.

'Every three seconds in one of the poorest countries in the world a child dies from extreme poverty. Every three seconds.'

He clicked his fingers in a slow rhythm to mark the timing of each death.

'Every three seconds somebody's son, somebody's daughter, someone's future is gone.

'Dead.

'With a stroke of a pen,' he concluded, 'eight men can make a difference and end the misery of millions of people.'

The crowd of almost a million people before him snapped their fingers too in a solemn participation in our world's responsibility for these deaths.

The star was visibly moved as the hundreds of thousands in the crowd held their hands aloft and clicked their fingers every three seconds. Before introducing the first act in the US concert, the Black Eyed Peas, Smith had to stand and compose himself.

At the side of the stage in London there were tears in the eyes of Lorna Dickinson. 'That was the world moment everyone has been waiting for,' she said, turning her attention back to the broadcasting technology and blinking back her tears.

'That has never happened before. It was technologically amazing. A global moment in which different part of the world talked to one another. How can we ignore Africa when its people can talk directly to us?'

Only Harvey seemed immune. He had received another message from the Royal Parks office reminding him of the end time. He had no patience with delays for television, even if 3.8 billion people were watching. 'Do that again,' he snarled at Lorna, 'and you're out of here.'

★ ★ ★

So what changed Bob Geldof's mind about doing another epic concert?

The Commission for Africa published its report, to general acclaim from both Africans and development specialists. At first Geldof was pleased.

But in the weeks that followed his fears steadily grew that the rich nations were not going to deliver on the comprehensive package which is what makes the Commission's recommendations different from all previous initiatives on Africa. The United States and Canada refused to sign up to the International Finance Facility which Gordon Brown had devised to finance the package. And Washington refused to agree to his plan to sell off some of the IMF's gold reserves to finance debt cancellation.

When Geldof's fellow campaigner, Bono, told the US Secretary of State, Condoleezza Rice, at a private meeting that during U2's tour of the States, that he would get 10,000 fans a night to call the White House, she simply replied: 'We can take the calls'.

As the days and weeks went by Geldof became steadily more depressed. The meeting of the G8 leaders at Gleneagles in Scotland in July was creeping steadily closer. And the deal on Africa was being blocked at every turn. The Americans were reluctant. The Germans and the Italians said they had no money. The Canadians were dragging their feet. The Japanese seemed immovable. Geldof brooded more and more. Had all that effort been wasted? How could these polititians be forced to act? How could you create the necessary 'domestic heat' to force them to respond? Curtis had pestered Geldof to do Live Aid 2 to focus the Make Poverty History campaign. Geldof's old friend from Dublin, Bono, wanted him to do another Live Aid for similar reasons. Uncovinced, Geldof would reply, 'You fucking do it then,' then the inevitable pause . . . 'Anyway it wouldn't work like that'. Still, the idea haunted him. It would be criminally irresponsible not to do something if it could make a difference. But in his head it didn't work. What was missing?

Then one morning he marched into the office of DATA, the lobby group on Africa which he and Bono work through. There was spring in his step.

'I think I've got it' he announced. 'Not Live Aid 2 but Live 8. Simultaneous concerts in London, Paris, Berlin, Rome, New York, Toronto, Tokyo, Moscow – one in each G8 country – at the end of which we ask everyone to get up and begin to walk to Gleneagles

Robbie Williams

to lobby the G8. Not The Long Walk to Freedom of Nelson Mandela's autobiography but a Long Walk to Justice. Because this is not Live Aid, it's not about charity. It's about what's right – political justice. We don't want their money. We want them.'

It was a mad, ambitious notion, which dwarfed all previous plans.

Calls were made to Live Aid veterans like U2, the Rolling Stones, Paul McCartney, Pete Townshend and Elton John and to a new generation including Coldplay, Oasis, Robbie Williams, the Stereophonics, the Darkness, Keane and Travis. And many more. Then the calls started to be returned. Bob's mobile began to permanently vibrate and overheat. Pink Floyd unbelievably would reform. So might The Cure. Maybe even the Spice Girls. 'The only person we haven't got is Elvis,' he said.

He rang Harvey Goldsmith, the impresario who did the original Live Aid. He travelled to Rome to get the Pope involved. He placed calls to various Hollywood stars to see if they would put their private jets at the disposal of campaigners wanting to fly across the Atlantic. He dreamt up the idea of a Dunkirk-like flotilla of little boats to ferry activists from Europe across the Channel. He asked Richard Branson for a free transatlantic plane and a train or two. He contacted ferry companies to ask for transport across the Channel for activists from Paris, Berlin and Rome. And bus and coach companies to set up transport within the UK.

Tony Blair's face was a picture the day that Bob told him what he was planning. He leaned forward in his seat, hands clasped, grip tightening imperceptibly as Geldof outlined some of the wheezes he had dreamt up. How he would get John Travolta, who is a pilot, to lead the flight – Hollywood jets across the Atlantic. How he had asked the round-the-world yachtswoman Dame Ellen MacArthur to lead the cross-Channel flotilla of little boats. How he was planning a flight by an old Dakota from Berlin as a symbolic reversal of the Berlin Airlift. On and on he went. Having galvanised the global political process through the Africa Comission, the plan was to arrest the attention of the global media for five weeks in the biggest educational awareness curve ever attempted. He was convinced that by 2nd July there would be one topic of conversation every pub, home, bus and taxi would talk with passion about – Africa.

And that's what happened. Geldof talked about getting a million people to Edinburgh. Only action on this scale could avoid another repetition of that long litany of G8 broken promises. Tony Blair's smile got more and more fixed, 'Gosh, Bob.' was all he could say.

As the logistics were explored various authorities put up objections to the use of certain parks, premises and facilities. To gain maximum impact Live 8 should be on 2nd July, the Saturday before the G8; that was not long enough to actually walk to Gleneagles. How could a million people be got there? Where would they sleep once they arrived?

The last and the trickiest of the Live 8 concerts to organise was the one in Moscow, for all the reasons you might suppose – plus one extra. One of the organisers was in conversation with a senior government official in the run-up to the event. The problem was, the apparatchik was told, that quite a few of the top Russian bands were just not available because of the short notice.

There was no turning back now. He had just six weeks to pull it all together. The Road to Gleneagles would not be easy, but the Long Walk to Justice had begun.

★ ★ ★

'The lesson today is how to die.'

Harvey Goldsmith, for all his worries about late-running, knew in his heart of hearts that there was no way he was keeping Bob Geldof off the stage. As Travis came off Bob and his band were waiting in the wings. Bob's partner, the French actress Jeanne Marine, hugged him as he went on, her face bursting with pride. At 5.37pm he was on stage.

The crowd in Hyde Park roared. 'I know it's cheeky,' he grinned half embarrassed, 'but I just had to play on this stage. I'm proud to be on this stage.' He sang just one song. Inevitably it was the Boomtown Rats' 'I Don't Like Mondays.' Inevitably because it is his song which is best known across the world. Inevitably because of its most famous line:

'The lesson today is how to die'.

It was the line which had stopped the show at Live Aid in 1985. A song written years before, after reading in a newspaper about a school massacre in the United States, had become charged with new meaning.

A new, even more terrible meaning.

He had stopped, his fist in the air, and allowed the world to think. And now, in 2005, in a different place, in a different world, he did the same thing again.

There was still a pregnancy in the pause. But it was different from before, and it was a different man who stood there, with his fist in the air. It was not just that the unlined face and the long brown hair had given way to features in which the years had etched their passing, or that the tangle of hair was now grizzled and on its way to being fully grey.

It was there in the eyes. In 1985 they had been filled with an uncomprehending horror, as well as a determination that something had to be done. This time the horror had gone, and in its place was the knowingness of a man who has learned that justice is harder than charity, but more essential. There was an irony in the eyes, but in an odd way this was a man who saw further than he did before.

In 1985 the arm had been crooked; twenty years on it was straight. At Live Aid he had felt that the threads of a lifetime were uniquely gathered in that one uplifted hand. It was something to do with destiny and purpose. At Live 8 he knew that history repeats itself, but that it could be a self-knowledge and an understanding of what is possible and what cannot be tolerated.

'Thanks for letting me do that,' he said at the end of the song.

'No, thank you, Bob,' the crowd, in the thunder of its applause, replied.

★ ★ ★

It was time for Brad Pitt to go on stage. He was to introduce Annie Lennox. But first there was the small matter of his speech. 'Come on,' said the make-up lady, 'I know it as well as you do now. I'll say it with you from back here.' He stepped forward. Even for a Hollywood star 200,000 upturned faces can be intimidating.

For many performers it is the pre-stage worry which ensures that they give their best when the moment comes. So it was for Brad Pitt. All those squats and breathing exercises worked. He gave what many in the crowd thought was the best speech of the day. 'Let us be outraged, let us be loud, let us be bold,' he told the crowd. And he was all those things as he spoke.

'Let us be the ones who say we do not accept that a child dies every three seconds simply because he does not have the drugs you and I have.

'Let us be the ones to say we are not satisfied that your place of birth determines your right to life. Let us be outraged, let us be loud, let us be bold.'

And he told a story, of how on his first trip to Africa he was startled by a young woman with Aids, a woman with children, who grabbed his arm and said "Please bring us the drugs, please help." He said: 'Let us be inspired by her, let us defend her, let us be fighters for her and the lives of her children whatever the cost, whatever it takes.

'We, the fortunate, let us remind each other this is what we stand for, this is who we are.'

The crowd cheered wildly as he left the stage and Annie Lennox arrived. She delivered a stunning set, including 'Why' played solo at the piano, with a film behind her of African people. Everyone in this film has Aids or HIV the caption read. Many of them are now dead.

By the time she was followed by UB40 the schedule by Harvey's desk was a full thirty minutes behind what had been planned. Another message from the Royal Parks. He was not sure what more he could do. His production team were achieving miracles, working with immense speed and intensity but without panic to turn around the acts. 'Do you realise how long it takes to turn around these acts – some of them the biggest names in the world – normally?' he said. 'About an hour. My guys are doing it in just four or five minutes.'

As Jerry Hall squeezed by him, looking for Bob, Harvey stormed over to the control desk. He pointed at Lorna from the BBC and Mitch the announcer.

'You're fired,' he shouted.

Lorna ignored him.

'You can't fire me,' said Mitch, 'because you're not paying me. I'm working for free.'

A little while later, after he had calmed down slightly, Harvey took the mike and went out on stage. 'We're going to run on till 10.30,' Harvey announced, 'so if people have connections to catch keep an eye on your watch'. What a nice mild-mannered considerate chap, they all thought.

The day passed in an increasing whirling blur. Madonna came off stage to be hugged by Geldof.

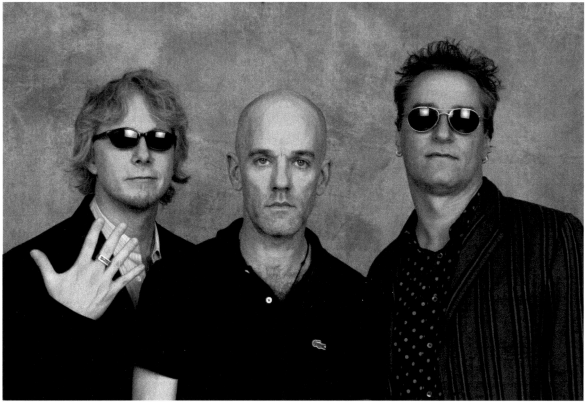

'Was I OK?' she asked, looking genuinely concerned that he might say she wasn't. But he didn't. She had been OK, he laughed.

As she moved off the dressing room she encountered Ricky Gervais who was still lurking around after having introduced REM and performed his 'Flashdance/MC Hammer fusion' dance routine from *The Office*. She told him he was her favourite comedian in the world, said she worshipped him and told him she would clean his floors for him. His reply was to look at her and say: 'Who are you?'

The government minister, Tessa Jowell, the Secretary of State for Culture, wandered by. She'd have a word with the Royal Parks, she said. That took the pressure off a bit.

So did the next person to lean across the control desk.

'Hi, I'm Paul McCartney's tour manager,' he said to Lorna from the BBC. 'Paul wants to drop a number. He'll leave out 'Follow Me'. He wants to keep the set up tempo.'

But by 8pm when The Killers took to the stage the show was running nearly an hour behind.

★ ★ ★

There is in the transition from Live Aid to Live 8 something more than a journey from charity to justice. There is a sense of one generation handing on the torch of compassion to the next. The new crowd seem determined not to let the flame flicker out.

Cynics have said that the younger bands said Yes to Live 8 simply because it was a great way of getting yourself in front of the biggest audience the world has ever seen. Marketing opportunities don't come much sweeter than that. Yet cynicism, as no less an organ of the establishment as The *Economist* put it in the week of Live 8, is only the most common form of naivety. 'Cynicism says more about the cynic than it does about people who find the idea of doing nothing intolerable,' said Travis's Fran Healy backstage. Indeed, overhear the conversations of many of the newer bands and their passion to make the world a better place is clear.

Snow Patrol's frontman Gary Lightbody was ten when he watched Live Aid. 'It made a big impression on me – mainly musical, but it also alerted me to the fact that there's a larger world out there. I certainly didn't grow up in a rich family, but we never went without dinner. So to see the devastation in Ethiopia gave me some early lessons in morality.'

To learn that 50,000 die from preventable diseases in our world every day is something he finds profoundly shocking. 'If it happened in this country there'd be a riot,' he said, backstage. 'It's a massive issue but the politicians wouldn't do anything if it wasn't for what is happening here today.'

Keane's piano man Tim Rice-Oxley acknowledged that he is 'a little star-struck by the line-up' but the band's real motivation goes much deeper. 'We're inspired by the grand ambition of the ideas behind it. The serious purpose is so massively important, and the opportunity to play even the tiniest part is something no one should refuse.'

Ms Dynamite agreed. 'How can you not be a part of something as important as this? Fame would be pointless if you didn't use it to support causes like Live 8.'

Dido took no persuading that raising money for charity was not the right response this time. 'I thought it was a really good idea to do something that was more about lobbying than fundraising, and it's already having an effect. People that didn't even know about the G8 are now talking about the summit and the prospect of dropping the debt. It's made it an everyday topic of conversation and I really do believe that's how massive changes happen.'

The announcements, no more than a month before Live 8, that European Union ministers have agreed to double aid and that the rich world's finance ministers have signed up to a $40 billion package of debt relief, is proof to Carl Dalermo from Razorlight that this 'amazing day' has had an impact even before a note was played. 'We've seen it already, with Blair and Co writing off debts for some of the poorest countries.'

Perhaps the most forceful of all the younger voices is Fran Healy. 'I've been to Africa and there's not a day goes by now without me thinking of the people I met there and what I can do. All the bands here today know why we're here and know the issues,' he said as he signed autographs in the artists' enclosure after his set.

'There are certain times in your life when you see things happening and you have to get involved. We have had to have a crash course in what it has taken

Bob Geldof twenty years to learn. But the lesson is that if enough people get involved anything can happen.'

The job after the concert will be to make sure that the G8 leaders deliver on the deal they sign up to. 'Politicians are the most slippery of all customers,' Fran Healy said. 'They are experts in denial, and their outrageous power is often matched only be their outrageous stupidity.'

Hold on, wasn't there something in the press about Geldof having asked the artists not to be rude about Blair and Bush? 'Can you imagine Geldof even saying that. Some paper made it up. He says the duty of an artist must be to say the truth about the world as he sees it.'

Travis is one of a number of bands putting their money, and their time, where their mouth is on this. When they have finished making their next record they plan to return to Sudan, where they made a documentary recently. 'Someone paid us £100,000 for doing a gig recently and we thought we'd use that money to fit out a drilling rig and go and dig some wells.'

★ ★ ★

Back on stage so many supermodels and other liggers are traipsing in and out that Harvey has introduced a shift system for backstage guests. Each artist could bring their mates and hangers-on into Harvey's precious three-foot margin to watch close-up, but when the set is finished each bunch is cleared unceremoniously.

Watching backstage is a bit of a mixed blessing. True, you can see people close up and rub shoulders with the celebs, but there is something odd about the whole experience. It's like watching the concert down the wrong end of a telescope. The acts are performing only a few yards away and, sideways on, they seem small and insignificant. It is as if it is in the distance, and only the frame of the screen lends the sense of scale, grandeur and history to the proceedings. Strikingly, throughout most of the concert Bob Geldof stood with his back to the acts, watching them on the BBC's TV monitors.

Waiting in the wings to see Sting come on next was Annie Lennox who is a comparatively old hand on matters African. She has for some time been an ambassador for Mandela's 46664 anti-Aids campaign.

'What goes on in Africa with the huge numbers of deaths from Aids is a kind of silent genocide,' she said.

'No one has united all these issues in the way this event has,' she said. 'But we can't just have a concert and walk away. We have to turn this moment into a movement, to translate awareness into activism, and I have a sense that is already happening.

'It's almost like destiny,' she added, 'like synchronicity.' As if he had taken his cue from the word, Sting struck up 'Every Breath You Take.'

Observant fans will have noticed an urgent, powerful Sting alter the words that day: 'Every game you play, till election day, every bond you break, every step you take, we'll be watching you'. Behind him flashed the pictures of the G8 leaders he was addressing.

He had mused on this earlier, sitting outside his dressing room. 'Twenty years on from Live Aid we're twenty years older and wiser. We know now that it's not just about us giving money. It's about creating infrastructure, which is the job of governments.'

What Live 8 had done, with its overt political message, backed by such numbers of people, he said, was create a new kind of mandate for politicians – one of such a size that they would ignore it at their peril.

'It's a new form of democracy. It's open to abuse of course but we have to work with that. It's our job as artists to be idealistic and optimistic. But it's important that we continue to scrutinise what happens afterwards, both with leaders here and in Africa. We're honour-bound now to follow through.'

As darkness fell an additional magic seemed to descend on the place. David Beckham sauntered out onto the stage to introduce Robbie Williams. The England football captain gazed around like a spectator stumbling across something remarkable in a clearing in a forest. He grinned boyishly, absorbing the applause for being Beckham, and showed no inclination to leave. It was as if he were in thrall to the 200,000 faces peering at him through the gloaming.

Robbie Williams looked like a man who didn't want to come off either. He gave a barnstorming performance which reminded fans what they had been missing since his last UK gig at Knebworth in 2003. In between he had clearly lost none of his ability to tease and manipulate a crowd like a master fisherman with an audience he had well and truly hooked.

His opener seemed to announce his intention to take on the mantle of the band who were twenty years ago dubbed 'the winners of Live Aid', Queen.

Williams began with 'We Will Rock You' segueing into 'Let Me Entertain You' and even slipping in the chorus from The Killers' 'All These Things That I've Done.' He concluded his brief set, after bending down with old-style showmanship to kiss a girl in the front row, with his anthem 'Angels,' recently voted the best song written in Britain in the past twenty five years. Few were surprised to learn later that his spot drew the biggest UK TV audience.

Beat that? On came The Who, angry, ageless old men still exploding with righteous indignation. Pete Townshend drew his guitar pick across the strings like a butcher drawing his knife through a carcass, and Roger Daltrey swung his microphone by the flex in a gigantic circle as of old. 'Who Are You?' as acerbic, pointed and relevant as ever and 'Won't Get Fooled Again' had lost none of its rage for being imbued with a new focused irony.

As they left the stage Townshend and Daltrey in turn embraced Geldof briefly. 'That was for you,' Townshend said to Geldof, who was speechless in front of one of his greatest heroes. 'I can't take in what's happening,' muttered Bob.

From out of the darkness dots of light appeared on the stage. They slowly turned into moons on the screen and, with no announcement, the wide spacey sound of Pink Floyd's first number, 'Breathe,' floated across the cool night air.

The tempo had changed. On stage the band were smiling at one another, half in delight, half in disbelief. There seemed to be tears in Roger Waters's eyes. Other eyes glistened among those watching at the side of the stage. It was as if the spirit of reconciliation of their reunion symbolised not just what Africa needed but also touched some spiritual ache within their fellow musicians. The crowd basked in the beauty of the moment, the music and the evening.

'I never thought I'd see this day,' said Geldof, in a voice tinged almost with a quiet ecstasy. 'They haven't spoken to each other for nearly twenty years,' he explained to his daughter Pixie.

Under the slogan 'No More Excuses' the band played 'Breathe' and then 'Money' with Roger Waters's celebrated bassline taking on a new poignancy. The slightly cerebral edge the Floyd had in the old days was softened, perhaps by the purpose of the day. Roger Waters even dedicated one song 'Wish You Were Here' to the band's lost genius founder Syd Barrett. Then came a gloriously expansive version of 'Comfortably Numb' from *The Wall*, the album that when turned into a film had one Bob Geldof play the lead role. As they left the stage they embraced.

'Pigs Have Flown,' read a banner in the crowd.

Geldof hugged them all as they left and made their way down the steep stairs from the stage. On the grass by the dressing rooms the magnificent old grey hairs could be seen soon after, touchingly exchanging phone numbers.

'The other bands all know why they're here,' said the drummer, Nick Mason. 'But for us there is the additional dimension. For Pink Floyd to reform after not playing for twenty years was something special,' he said, quiet understatement being the English way.

★ ★ ★

There was a reporter from the *Sun* who took Bob Geldof literally. The Long Walk to Justice, Bob had called it, in homage to Nelson Mandela's *Long Walk to Freedom*. The tabloid journo worked out how long it would take to get there – from London to Gleneagles, that is – and set out in good time.

Bob, by contrast, took the train, and walked up and down the carriages a bit. 'It's a metaphor, you prat, you don't actually have to walk,' was his riposte to those of a literal frame of mind. It was making the journey that was the point.

And he encouraged people to get to Edinburgh in whatever way he could. Some came by car, others by boat, others by coach, others by plane.

Two days after Live 8 Geldof was at Heathrow early in the morning to greet a planeload of protesters who had just been flown in – free of charge, courtesy of Virgin Airways – from the United States, one hundred in total, two from each of the states of the union.

The day after he himself joined a train – also laid on free by his old mate Richard Branson's Virgin – from London to Edinburgh.

On the train to Edinburgh with him travelled the Hollywood movie stars Susan Sarandon and

Tim Robbins. George Clooney later flew in to join them. Among the other passengers were the handful of intrepid yatchsmen who had set out, at Geldof's impulsive instigation, across the channel in what he dubbed Sail 8. The train contained activists from fifty four different countries, including one who had spent three days travelling from Mali.

It was all beginning to work. Africa was getting great play in the media in countries like the United States and Germany which had between ignoring the issue. The attitudes of the civil servants from Washington and Berlin had changed inside the backroom meetings designed to pave the way for an agreement at Gleneagles. Things which had previously been off the agenda were suddenly up for discussion.

At the same time a constituency of activists who arose would be prepared to keep up the pressure to make sure the politicians delivered on whatever they pledged.

Finally, nine and a half hours after he opened the extraordinary day, Paul McCartney returned to the Live 8 stage with his own band to close the show.

'I remember you lot from this morning,' he joshed to the audience and launched into a coruscating set of timeless Beatles classics beginning with 'Get Back'.

For the second number George Michael ran out, provoking a gasp from the audience. Their duet had been trailed but Michael's appearance was a delightful surprise to many in the crowd. They sang 'Baby You Can Drive My Car' from *Rubber Soul* before slamming the finale into total rock with a reclaimed 'Helter Skelter', a 1968 hallucinogenic anthem which had acquired sinister overtones after its adoption by Charles Manson. No more. Tonight it sounded like the progenitor of heavy metal.

'From wherever you are to Edinburgh' read the legend above the stage as the concert closed with a mass rendition of the refrain from 'Hey Jude'. Most of the day's performers joined McCartney on stage to sing.

It was not long before midnight. The concert had lasted ten hours. But the Live 8 day had lasted even longer, beginning in Tokyo at 6am ending in Barrie,

Ontario nineteen hours later.

It had been, said Bob Geldof, one magnificent day.

★ ★ ★

It was the first morning of the G8 summit in Gleneagles. The eight most powerful men in the world were assembling through the day in a five-star hotel on a golf course in the beautiful rolling hills of lowland Scotland. That night the presidents and prime ministers would begin the formal proceedings by dining with the Queen of England. But first they had to receive some other visitors.

Bob Geldof, Bono and Richard Curtis boarded a helicopter to fly into the centre of a high-security zone, much as they had done on the morning of Live 8. Only this time they were part of a delegation – along with Mike Aaronson of the Make Poverty History coalition and the Kenyan Nobel Prize winner Wangari Maathai – to meet the summit's chairman, Prime Minister Tony Blair.

In addition to the official meeting, the two musicians had a private forty minute session with the US President George Bush, and a shorter meeting with the German Chancellor, Gerhard Schroeder – the leaders of the two nations thought most likely to obstruct a good deal for Africa.

What they found surprised them. President Bush told the pair that he had watched the Live 8 broadcasts. 'The most moving moment', he said, 'was when Birhan, the child who had appeared at death's door in a film at the Live Aid concert in 1985, came out,' Geldof said. 'It clearly reminded him that when politicians negotiate in the rarefied atmosphere of a place like Gleneagles there are individuals like her who live or die by their decisions.'

The two Irish rock singers were unprepared for the level of engagement with Africa the US President demonstrated. 'His two daughters have been working there and his wife, Laura – who was at the meeting – is about to tour Africa,' Geldof said. 'And she is particularly concerned with the education of girls.'

Girls are far less likely than boys to go to school in Africa, in part because of cultural gender biases. But it is also for reasons which aid could rectify. 'He was clearly struck by the fact that many girls will not go to school merely because they lack separate

toilet facilities,' said Geldof. 'When they have a menstrual period they stay at home for a week every month because schools have no proper toilet facilities. Free school meals make it economically beneficial to send daughters to school. Or costs less than feeding them at home.'

Bono pressed the President to add further to the increases in aid to Africa which Washington pledged in the run-up to Live 8 – but which was short of what was needed to raise the additional $25 billion a year recommended by the Commission for Africa.

On trade, the pair also secured from the US leader a commitment to fix a date to end subsidies on agricultural exports by rich countries, which make it impossible for many African farmers to scrape a living. President Bush said he would be happy to agree a date to be included in the next day's closing communiqué, provided European leaders did the same.

Chancellor Schroeder told the two musicians that he would stick to his commitment to increase aid to 0.56 per cent of Germany's national income by 2010. But the Live 8 campaigners remained stony-faced at the press conference and photocall which followed. 'Smiles might have been premature,' said Geldof. 'They can wait until tomorrow for those.'

The two campaigners then took their helicopter straight to Edinburgh's Murrayfields stadium where a final Live 8 midweek eve-of-summit concert had begun with the Scots heroes The Proclaimers singing their old hit '500 Miles' with lyrics altered to reflect the journey from London to Edinburgh and the Long Walk to Justice.

Not long after he got back Bono came out onto the stage carrying an unlikely looking object – a briefcase – which he put down by the side of the microphone like a man coming home from the office.

'So I just came back from the most famous golf course in the world at Gleneagles. I met with these powerful men but I want you to know,' he said, leaning into the microphone as if to speak confidentially to the stadium's 60,000 crowd, 'I did not play golf. I told them they can play golf but they can't play poker, the stakes are too high. There's too many lives at stake. I hope you don't mind but I gave them your permission to spend your money. . . ending extreme poverty in our lifetime. They wanted to know where did I get the authority to

say that and I held up this box,' he said, raising the briefcase for the audience to see.

'In this box are the signatures of the thirty eight million people who are ready to go to work on this issue, and that's just the Live 8 campaign. When you add to that 157 million people who signed up for the Global Action Against Poverty in seventy five countries, I would call that permission to spend your money. That's the most powerful mandate in the history of mandates.'

The crowd roared its approval. And they did so again later on when Bob Geldof came out to speak and addressed the G8 leaders directly. 'You asked us to engage in this process and we engaged. We came to Murrayfield tonight with 3.8 billion people – the number who signed their support for Live 8 – in our back pockets. Should you fail we will not be cynical, we will bide our time and when you come to us and ask for our approval at the ballot box, we will tell you to Fuck Off!' The crowd sent up a wild roar of agreement.

Two days later G8 leaders signed the biggest aid deal in Africa's history, agreeing to double the amount which had been given in 2004 over the next six years.

That was not all. They endorsed the deal agreed by their finance ministers as part of the build-up to the summit to write off $40 billion of debt. That means fourteen African countries will not have to pay any of the billions of debt they owe the big international banks like the International Monetary Fund.

On trade they agreed to end the export subsidies which allow the West to dump excess produce on global markets ruining the livelihoods of African farmers, though they will not fix a date until December 2005 as suggested in the Commission for Africa report. More significantly, the summit agreed that African countries should no longer be forced to open up their markets to Western imports, or follow economic policies dictated by the rich world, in return for aid.

But overall the message was clear. In the words of Kofi Annan the UN Secretary General 'This has been, without doubt,' he said, 'the greatest G8 summit there has ever been for Africa'.

Many aid agencies said the deal was not good enough. Doubling aid by 2010 was too slow. The debt deal applied to too few countries, and had too many conditions attached. And on trade there were only words.

This disagreement was, in part, because the focus of the development agencies was on world poverty, whereas Live 8, as Geldof had made consistently clear, if even simply through it's logo, was focusing specifically on Africa.

The plan set out in the Commission for Africa, which Tony Blair set up at Geldof's behest, had been largely fulfilled.

The Commission said: double aid by 2010, and that has been done. Marks: ten out of ten, was the Geldof verdict.

The Commission said: cancel one hundred per cent of mulitlateral debt. That has been done for fourteen countries at once, with another eighteen on the way. Marks: eight out of ten, (a bit less because some of the harmful conditions attached to debt cancellation remain in place).

Trade was harder to mark. There was a glimmer of a breakthrough but in the end no date was set for the end of export subsidies. African states, the communiqué promised, will no longer be forced to open up their markets to Western goods. And – though not many people noticed it – there was a lot of support in the aid package which will help Africa to produce more of what it needs to trade, and at the right price, for this is as big a constraint on Africa trading as are Western trade barriers.

Almost fifty of the things the Commission for Africa report called for had been delivered. The communiqué commits governments to:

- double research spending on Aids and provide virtually universal access to anti-Aids treatment for all those who need it by 2010.
- increase action against malaria to reach eighty five per cent of vulnerable populations by 2015.
- provide anti-Aids drugs to nine million Africans within the next six years.
- give all children access to free and compulsory primary education.
- support for Africa's higher education institutions.
- support for important African initiatives, such as the African Union's peer review mechanism and its New Partnership for Africa (NEPAD) programme.
- fight corruption with measures to make African governments more accountable to their people.

Get the rich nations to:
- implement the UN Convention on Corruption.
- identify and freeze the assets of corrupt African leaders which are deposited in Western banks.
- return looted cash to its rightful owners.
- clamp down on Western companies who pay bribes.
- train and equip 20,000 more African soldiers as peacekeepers.
- impose restrictions on the trade in small arms that is largely controlled from Europe.

The G8 and African leaders reckon that the measures they have agreed could double the size of Africa's economy and trade by 2015.

'Only time will tell if this is a historic summit,' Geldof said. 'What is true is that people have forced a change of policy onto the global agenda. Today gives Africa the opportunity of beginning to end poverty over the next ten years.'

Bono agrees. 'We jumped up and down when Live Aid raised a total of $200m in 1985. Now Live 8 and its call for justice has raised $25bn in new money.'

What does that mean to the poorest of the poor?

It means 600,000 children will not die from malaria every year.

It means anti-Aids drugs will save more than nine million lives.

It means polio can be eradicated in Africa.

It means twenty million more children will go to school.

It means five million more orphans will be cared for and it goes on.

These are not merely numbers. Each one of them could grow up to be like that young Ethiopian woman, Birhan Woldu, who almost died on camera at the Live Aid concert in 1985 and who walked onto the stage a beautiful, confident, dignified twenty four year-old agricultural student at Live 8.

Twenty years ago the world watched her and cried. Last week the world could not stop smiling.

★ ★ ★

Then, all at once, it was finished, an hour and a half later than planned. The darkness was still and the adrenaline began to ebb. Hyde Park was silent. Live 8 was over. Musicians, technicians and activists drifted aimlessly into the night. The backstage bar had

run out of booze. The after-show party in Regent Street seemed too wearingly far away.

Bob Geldof and Richard Curtis sat in a production office with the remnants of a bottle of wine. Mariah Carey stuck her head round the door. 'Anyone want to go clubbing?'

'I don't think so, love,' said Bob. He smiled and thanked her for everything. 'I think I'll go home.'

'Of course,' she beamed back.

'Are you not going to get changed before you go?' said Bob, the father of four daughters. Mariah was still wearing the small black number laced tightly at the sides that she had worn during the show.

'Well I do have my blue dress, but that's kinda more revealing,' she smiled sweetly.

'OK,' laughed Bob. 'Off you go.'

A tall slightly-stooping sandy haired man came into the room with his daughter and her friend.

'John!' shouted Geldof, and rose to give him a long intense hug. This was John Kennedy. No one in the crowd would have recognised him had he gone out on the stage an hour earlier. But this was the man without whom none of it could have happened.

Kennedy was a record business lawyer. He just happened to be in the room twenty years before when Bob walked in to see someone else, ablaze with the idea for the first Band Aid record. 'You'll be needing someone to do the legal stuff,' he had said at the end of the conversation. 'I'll do it if you like.'

He did it. And all the nightmare contract work for the Live Aid concert which followed. Since then John Kennedy has been the key man with Geldof in running the Band Aid charity trust. And now he had quietly, unobtrusively as ever, done the work of a titan behind the scenes on Live 8. Over the years in which he has had a job as president of Universal Music International and now as the head of the music industry's anti-bootleg and piracy watchdog his role had grown from that of lawyer to that of almost 'executive producer'. John Kennedy, OBE, was the man who made it all work.

'You had a good day?' Geldof asked him.

'It's been . . . just amazing. You?'

'Just. . . amazing! Couldn't have done it without you though.'

Kennedy just smiled shyly. 'This man,' said Geldof,

to the rest of the room, 'is the rock on which Live 8 was built.'

'There's one place with some booze left,' someone said.

'Where?'

'McCartney's dressing room.'

It turned out that the former Beatle was high on his performance to the biggest audience the world had ever seen. He was in full flight about a row he'd had with a taxi driver before the gig. 'I said to him "It's a great cause." He said: "Yes and No." I said to him: "What's the No bit?". He said: "Well our pensioners could do with the money." So I said to him: "But hold on, think about the millions of children in Africa born with debt around their necks – and that 50,000 people somewhere in the world die of easily preventable diseases every day. . . If that was happening in England we'd sort it pretty damn quick."' The message was out there, and continuing to spread.

'I just don't think it is possible', concluded McCartney, 'that the politicians can ignore the will of the people that has been displayed today.'

Geldof took a glass of red wine. But even the company of a childhood hero could not tempt him for long. 'I'm all in,' he said, with a triumphant weariness. 'I think I'll just go home.'

'Give us a ring if you need me in another twenty years,' shouted the former Beatle.

'I don't think so,' called back Bob Geldof, over his shoulder. 'Somehow I don't think so.'

THE BAND
OF THE
COLDSTREAM
GUARDS
FANFARE

'Let this be absolutely clear before the first note is played. Everyone taking part in these concerts is there because the many millions watching will not tolerate the further pain of the poor while we have the financial and moral means to prevent it'
– Bob Geldof

PAUL MCCARTNEY AND U2
SGT. PEPPER'S LONELY HEARTS CLUB BAND

'I must admit I blub quite a bit and I blubbed when Paul and Bono kicked off – you want great rock'n'roll moments? That's a great rock and roll moment! Everyone around me – people like Bill Gates and Kofi Annan looked like something had punched them – they just turned away and started to blub. I just felt that everything that rock and roll had ever promised or I had ever imagined it to be as a kid had been made real on that stage'
– Bob Geldof

'Molecules in the air round here are vibrating a little faster than normal' – **Bono**

U2
IT'S A BEAUTIFUL DAY, VERTIGO, ONE, UNCHAINED MELODY

'This is amazing'
– The Edge

'This is our moment. This is our time. This is our chance to stand up for what's right. We're not looking for charity, we're looking for justice. We can't fix every problem, but the ones we can fix, we must.' – **Bono**

'Did that really just happen?'

Bono

MAKUHARI MESSE, TOKYO, **JAPAN**

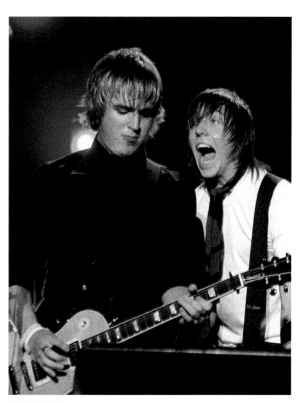

GOOD CHARLOTTE

MCFLY

BJÖRK

'I see people starving, I am crying.
I'm a total mess'

COLDPLAY
IN MY PLACE, BITTERSWEET SYMPHONY (WITH RICHARD ASHCROFT), FIX YOU

'Bob Geldof is a hero of our time'
– Chris Martin

PET SHOP BOYS

RED SQUARE, MOSCOW, RUSSIA

'As we arrived, dressed as Lou and Andy, we bumped into Paul McCartney and a gaggle of photographers. We posed together and I just thought We're having our photo taken with Macca. We're having our photo taken with Macca. Oh my God. Does it get any better than this? I couldn't see much onstage as I was wearing strong glasses. As just a fat little comic I felt very privileged to be there.' **– Matt Lucas**

'There are so many negative, things at the moment, this is a positive step' – Elton John

ELTON JOHN
THE BITCH
IS BACK,
SATURDAY
NIGHT'S
ALRIGHT FOR
FIGHTING,
CHILDREN
OF THE
REVOLUTION
(WITH PETE
DOHERTY)

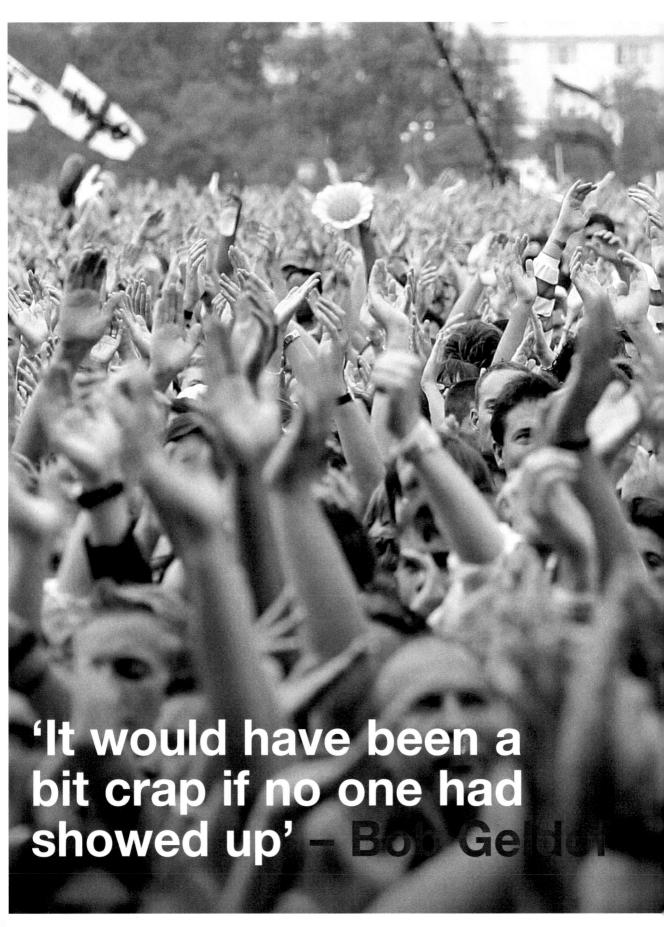

'It would have been a bit crap if no one had showed up' – Bob Geldof

'I'm honoured to be taking part. I just want to play my guitar and hopefully it helps. I may mumble a lot down the microphone on stage, but when I sing it's from my heart'
— Pete Doherty

'Today this is a Declaration of Inter-Dependence. We're all in this together' – Will Smith, Philadelphia

WILL SMITH

MUSEUM OF ART, PHILADELPHIA, USA

'Some day in the future all people, no matter where they are born will be able to lead a healthy life. We can do this and when we do, it will be the best thing that humanity has ever done' **– Bill Gates**

DIDO
WHITE FLAG, THANK YOU, SEVEN SECONDS (WITH YOUSSOU N'DOUR)

'There are millions
and millions of voices,
asking you to do the
right thing and we
will be waiting' – Dido

'I see myself in the role of an ambassador portraying the reality and the real message of Africa and I have to be here and put a hundred percent effort into supporting it. Africans feel proud of what the music industry is doing now to try to help to push people to make a decision. Live8 is different from what has gone before as it's much more about a message than raising money'
– Youssou N'Dour

BRYAN ADAMS
'I'm here 20 years later.
Bob Geldof has done an incredible job'

BARRIE, TORONTO, CANADA

DEEP PURPLE

TOMMY LEE   **NEIL YOUNG**

THE STEREOPHONICS
DAKOTA, SUPERMAN, LOCAL BOY IN THE PHOTOGRAPH

'It doesn't take much for a band to sing a few songs and help bring awareness that'll help suffering in the world. Long live rock 'n' roll!'
– Kelly Jones, Stereophonics

'You'd think my single lasting memory would be a quarter of a million people screaming at me to 'do The Dance' but it was actually Brad Pitt and Madonna telling me they were fans. I think it was because I looked so cool in slightly-too-short-for-me sweat pants and t-shirt. I like to make an effort for the biggest TV audience ever.'
– Ricky Gervais

REM
EVERYBODY HURTS,
MAN ON THE MOON,
IMITATION OF LIFE

'Hello – this is what we do.'
– Michael Stipe, REM

'This really is the
United Nations.
The whole world
has come together
in solidarity with
the poor. On behalf
of the poor, the
voiceless and the
weak, I thank you.'
– Kofi Annan

MS DYNAMITE
DY-NA-MI-TEE-HEE, REDEMPTION SONG

'We are a nation that has tortured and killed the Third World for centuries. If there's a debt to be paid, surely we're the ones who owe it. I would bet my life that if 50,000 people died in the western world today, something would be done by this evening to make sure it didn't happen again tomorrow' – **Ms Dynamite**

KEANE
SOMEWHERE ONLY WE KNOW, BEDSHAPED

'We want to let our leaders know that we are the generation that refused to turn a blind eye to this tragedy'
– Tim Rice-Oxley, Keane

TRAVIS
SING, TURN, STAYING ALIVE, WHY DOES IT ALWAYS RAIN ON ME?

'I am happy to say we know everyone here. It's like school or a family thing. Paul McCartney's not the Grandad because he can still kick like a mule – he's actually the Father. You've also got Bono who is sort of our cool Uncle and the rest of us are like kids running about playing chasing games – it's great.'
– Fran Healy, Travis

ALICIA KEYS

**DAVID
MATTHEWS
BAND**

**MUSEUM OF ART,
PHILADELPHIA, USA**

'The lesson today is how to die. Still'
– Bob Geldof

'Look busy, it's the boss'

– BBC DJ announcing Bob

BOB GELDOF
I DON'T LIKE MONDAYS

'I am withering in my scorn for those who say it's not going to work. Even if it doesn't work, what do they propose? Every night forever watching people dying on our TV screens?' **– Bob Geldof**

MARY FITZGERALD SQUARE, JOHANNESBURG

'Sometimes it falls upon
a generation to be great.
You can be that great generation.'
– Nelson Mandela, Johannesburg

'By the time this concert has ended, 30,000 Africans will have died from poverty. This time tomorrow it will be another 30,000. Let us be outraged. Let us be loud. Let us be bold.'
– Brad Pitt

'Cynics say it's pointless.
Fuck them. To do nothing
is totally unacceptable.'
– Annie Lennox

ANNIE LENNOX
WHY, LITTLE BIRD, SWEET DREAMS

'We are here today to urge the leaders of the G8 summit to take action for the people of Africa and all the nations where poverty and despair are a way of life. Everyone of us believes that this is a righteous cause. Together with focus and determination we can all begin to make poverty history'
– Annie Lennox

'Today is a pebble that has
been thrown into a pond that
has been lying stagnant and
its ripples will go wide'
– Annie Lennox

BLACK EYED PEAS

UB40
MEDLEY INCLUDING FOOD FOR THOUGHT, RED RED WINE, WHO YOU FIGHTING FOR?

'The message to the G8 is: pull your finger out. We've had enough.'
– Ali Campbell, UB40

SNOOP DOGG
UPS AND DOWNS, IT'S A G THANG, DROP IT, SIGNS, WHAT'S MY NAME

'There's a lot of rich people in the world and a lot of them are just selfish. We are saying we don't want it to be like that any more'
– Snoop Dogg

STEVIE WONDER

JAY-Z

'We're making a difference in the
world, not just for a moment but
forever… I'm sure that from heaven
above… the Almighty is smiling
at the contribution of tonight. The
only way that we can end hate is to
give more love'

'I don't remember Live Aid because I was too young. But today isn't about 20 years ago, it is about now. 20,000 children are dying every day as a result of poverty. We're here to put pressure on the G8 to come away with a result, not more broken fucking promises.'
— Johnny Borrell, Razorlight

RAZORLIGHT
SOMEWHERE ELSE, GOLDEN TOUCH, VICE

'All you need is love. John Lennon said that. Music can change the world. Bono said that. Sign the fucking petition. I said that.'
– Johnny Borrell, Razorlight

BON JOVI

DESTINY'S CHILD

BEYONCÉ

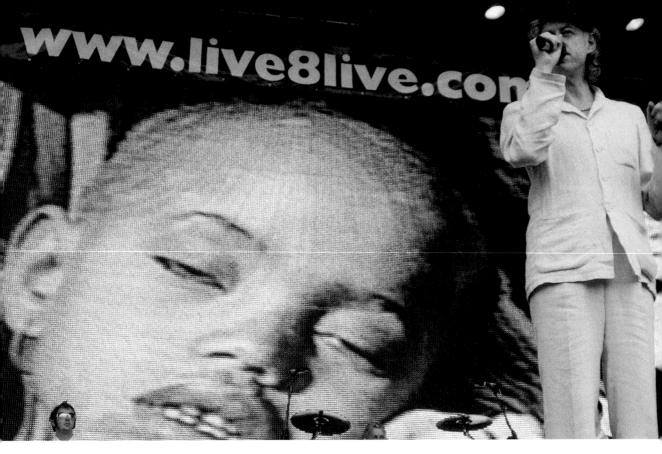

'Some of you were here twenty years ago. Some of you weren't even born. I wanted to show you why we started this long, long walk to justice. Don't let them tell you this doesn't work. Who is this beautiful woman? This little girl had 10 minutes to live 20 years ago. Because we did a concert, last week she did her agricultural exams at her school in the northern Ethiopian highlands. Don't let them tell you this doesn't work.'
– **Bob Geldof**

'Hello from Africa. We Africans love you very much.' – Birhan Woldu

MADONNA WITH THE LONDON COMMUNITY GOSPEL CHOIR
LIKE A PRAYER, MUSIC, RAY OF LIGHT

'This is a day of joy, hope, optimism and life for those who have none.'
– Bob Geldof

SNOW PATROL
CHOCOLATE, RUN

'You can't say no to Bob – he's a legend. The run up to the G8 summit is the most important political event in our generation's history. Today it is coupled with the biggest musical event in our generation.'
– Gary Lightbody, Snow Patrol

THE KILLERS
ALL THESE THINGS THAT I'VE DONE

'There was only one song of ours we could do: All These Things That I've Done. We've got soul but we're not soldiers.'
– Brandon Flowers, The Killers

PALAIS DE VERSAILLES, **FRANCE**

THE CURE
'There's too much anger for things to just remain as they are'
– Robert Smith

PLACEBO

SHAKIRA

JOSS STONE
I HAD A DREAM, SUPER DUPER LOVE, SOME KIND OF WONDERFUL

SCISSOR SISTERS
LAURA, TAKE YOUR MAMA, EVERYBODY WANTS THE SAME THING

'Sign the petition and write to a politician!'
– Ana Matronic, Scissor Sisters

CIRCUS MAXIMUS, ROME, ITALY

'This was an important concert –
maybe ever better than Live Aid'
– Simon Le Bon, Duran Duran

DURAN DURAN

FAITH HILL

TIM MCGRAW

JOVANOTTI

VELVET REVOLVER
DO IT FOR THE KIDS, FALL TO PIECES, SLITHER

'Guns N' Roses were just forming when Live Aid was on. We were rehearsing in this windowless basement and didn't even have a TV. I was just a scrawny punk rock kid and guess I still am, but it's great to be part of this not just cos we respect the other performers, but because it's the right thing to do.'
– Duff McKagan, Velvet Revolver

'We'll be watching you'
– Sting

STING
MESSAGE IN A
BOTTLE, DRIVEN TO
TEARS, EVERY
BREATH YOU TAKE

MARIAH CAREY
VISION OF LOVE, HERO, WE BELONG TOGETHER

'I felt close to the people out there and being on stage with the African Children's Choir was a brilliant moment for me – they represent 11 million orphaned children in Africa. They are survivors.'
– **Mariah Carey**

BRIAN WILSON

BRANDENBURG GATE, BERLIN, **GERMANY**

GREEN DAY

FAITHLESS
A-HA

ROXY MUSIC

'I am sure this is inspiring for me and all of you. We are so lucky to be involved in a day like this. You have been absolutely fantastic all day, and I am sure you will carry on into the night.'
– David Beckham

ROBBIE WILLIAMS
WE WILL ROCK YOU,
LET ME ENTERTAIN
YOU, FEEL, ANGELS

'This is brilliant!'
– Robbie Williams

THE WHO
WHO ARE YOU?
WON'T GET
FOOLED AGAIN

'There's something about the Floyd that always makes you question your life. Seeing them together was one of the greatest moments of the evening.'
– Bob Geldof

PINK FLOYD
BREATHE, MONEY, WISH YOU WERE HERE, COMFORTABLY NUMB

'It seemed like a good opportunity to have a small victory over rancour.'
– Roger Waters

'When we all sat down together again for this reunion we eyed each other in a slightly alarmed kind of way, but I think but we are all reasonably grown-up now and we are quite a bit older than when we last played together. It was an interesting moment when we got the call from Bob, as I thought I was going to be on a hiding to nothing. Then I thought I couldn't possibly live with myself if I had the opportunity to do something like this and I didn't do it.'

– Nick Mason

'This is a
moment that
could change
the world'
– Paul
McCartney

PAUL McCARTNEY
GET BACK, DRIVE MY CAR (WITH GEORGE MICHAEL), HELTER SKELTER, THE LONG AND WINDING ROAD, HEY JUDE (ALL-STAR FINALE)

'There's no doubt about what today is all about. You don't have to force it down people's throats – they see it, they are out there watching it.'
– Midge Ure

'We know what to do. There isn't a plan B. Plan B is that we continue to watch them die.'

'After it is all over I want you to stand back and say "what have we just been part of?" and to conclude this is for one aim – to alter the structure of poverty in this world for ever.'
– Bob Geldof

WITH CO-ORGANISERS RICHARD CURTIS & EMMA FREUD

'Live8 was the most extraordinary global collective moment. A louder or clearer message could not have been sent to the key 8 politicians. The world is in unison – we demand an end to the injustices of the world.'
– Harvey Goldsmith

'All we are saying is give people an equal chance to lead good, healthy lives. Let's hope that as a result of this long day, more will.'
– Richard Curtis

'It has been a glorious and magnificent day, a day of hope, possibility and life for those who have none'
– Bob Geldof

Acknowledgements

UK
Bob Geldof – Live 8 Producer
Harvey Goldsmith CBE – Live 8 Producer
John Kennedy – Live 8 Producer
Richard Curtis – Executive Producer
Kevin Wall – Executive Producer TV/Worldwide
Bono – Consultant to Live 8
Emma Freud – Associate Producer
Emma Parry – Associate Producer
Mark Krais and Richard Bray – Legal Advisors,
Kieran Jay, Ailish McMahon, Annette O'Sullivan, Robyn Bradshaw, Robin Davis, Jill Sinclair Joe Cannon, Maggie Gonzalez, James Aston – BDO Stoy Hayward Pat Savage and John Horwood – Accountants, O J Kikenny and Co
Bernard Doherty – Public Relations, LD Publicity
Matthew Freud – Special Advisor/Associate Producer Freud Communications – Public Relations Support

For Harvey Goldsmith Productions Ltd
Diana Goldsmith – Artist Liaison
Debbie Scorah – Ticketing and Marketing Manager
Tommy Tyekiff – Assistant to Harvey Goldsmith
Catherine Carnie – Support to Harvey Goldsmith
Nancy Skipper – Work Permits
Rashida Dhawan – Financial Controller
Sarah Barrett – Office Assistant

Live 8 Production
Steve Allen – Production Director, Entertee Productions Ltd
Julie Chennells – Production Co-ordinator
Peter Bingemann – Set Designer
Mickey Curbishley – Director of Sales for Lighting, PRG Europe
Yvonne Donnelly Smith – Account Executive for PRG Europe – Lighting
Peter Barnes – Lighting Director
Bryan Grant – Head Of Live Audio, Brittania Row
Mike Lowe – Pre-Production, Britannia Row
John Gibbon – Crew Chef,

Britannia Row Britannia Row
Andrew Robinson – FOH Engineer, Britannia Row
Mark Ballard – FOH Engineer, Britannia Row
Chris Coxhead – FOH Engineer, Britannia Row
Dave Bracey – Console Programmer, Britannia Row
Dave Webster – FOH Technician, DIGICO
Robert Andrews – FOH Technician, DIGICO
Chris Morrison - Audio Designer/Engineer, Britannia Row
Jonathon Lewis – Motor Engineer, Britannia Row
Maurizio Gennarri – Motor Engineer, Britannia Row
Robert Doyle – Monitor Technician, DIGICO
Roger Wood – Monitor Technician, DIGICO
Peter Mcglynn – Stage Audio Chief, Britannia Row
Mark Isbister – Stage Audio, Britannia Row
Nick Maddren – Stage Audio, Britannia Row
Stephanie Thompson – Stage Audio, Britannia Row
Robert Elliot – Stage Audio, Britannia Row
Steve Donavan – Stage Audio, Britannia Row
Aron Ross – Stage Audio, Britannia Row
Shane Ryan – Stage Audio, Britannia Row
Andrew Burch – Stage Audio, Britannia Row
Andrew Andreou – Stage Audio, Britannia Row
Amanda Thomson – Stage Audio, Britannia Row
Josh Lloyd – Stage Audio, Britannia Row
Johnny Dodkin – Stage Audio, Britannia Row
Richard Trow - PA Technician, Britannia Row
Bob Lopez – PA Design/Technician, Britannia Row
Joseph Taffner – PA Technician, Electrovoice
Jock Bain – PA Technician, Britannia Row
Nico Royan – PA Technician, Britannia Row
James Bowyer – PA Technician, Britannia Row
Andy Reed – PA Technician, Britannia Row
Gordon Lilley – PA Technician, Britannia Row
Peter Russell – PA Technician, Britannia Row

Franz Lang – PA Technician, Electrovoice
Barry Mccloud – Radio Technician, Britannia Row
Dave Hawker – Radio Technician, Sennheiser
Andrew Lilywhite – Radio Technician, Sennheiser
Jerry Wing – Mains power, Britannia Row
Richard Walsh – Stage Comms, Britannia Row
Richard Williamson – Stage Comms, Britannia Row
Roger Barrett – Staging, Star Events Group
Phil Broad – Head Rigger, Star Events Group
Martin Fredericks – Artist Liaison
Steve Jones – Stage Manager, Stage Miracles
Frenchie – Set Structure, Steel Monkies
Tony Ball – Security, Show and Event Security
Mark Hamilton – Security, Rock Steady
Simon Battersby – Security, ShowSec
Dave Crump – Screens, CT Screenco
Kevin Williams – Director of Live Screen Footage
Richard Shipman – Director of Screen Graphics
Kim Davenport – Artist Catering, Eat Your Hearts Out
Vicki Huxel – Artist Catering, Eat Your Hearts Out
Kate Prince – Crew Catering, Eat To The Beat
Mark Fuller – Catering
Graeme Dixon – Furniture/ Ambience, GLD
Nu Nu – Backline/ Risers, MusicBank
Paul Bissoni – Backline Transportation Manager
Marwan Khalek – Aviation Co-ordinator, Gama Aviation Ltd
Andy Airfix – Logo Design, Satori
Rob Farrar – Logo Design, Satori
Byron Carr – Music By Appointment
Beaker and Mark – Stage Banners & Scrims, Impact
Tim Cox – Passes and Accreditation, Publicity and Display

Hyde park arena event management
Clear Channel Entertainment (Music) UK
Stuart Galbraith – Event Director

John Probyn – Event Manager
Hannah Blake – Event Co-ordinator
Sarah Woodhead – Hospitality Manager
And all CCE staff and contractors
Anton Jeffery – Ten Alps Events
Danny Oakes & David Bell – Merchandise, Firebrand Live Ltd

BBC Television
Executives in Charge of Production:
Jana Bennett
Alan Yentob
Peter Fincham
Presenters:
Jonathan Ross
Graham Norton
Fern Cotton
Jo Whiley
Technical Manager:
Christopher C. Bretnall
Producers:
Cerrie Frost
Kim Ross
Directors:
Claire Popplewell
Geoff Posner
Richard Valentine
Executive Producers:
Lorna Dickinson Elaine Paterson
Executive Editor:
Nick Vaughan-Barratt

World broacast
Paul Flattery – World Broadcast Producer
Elizabeth Flowers – World Broadcast Associate Producer
Andy Brilliant – World Television Sales
John Rubey – Director of World Broadcast Distribution & Broadcaster Services
Jeff Pollack – World Radio Executive Producer
Tommy Hadges & Tommy Nast – World Radio Producers
Brooke Gardner – Production Coordinator
Liz Heller – Advisor online marketing
Nancy Smalley – Support to Kevin Wall
Jonah Reynolds & Laurice Rothenburg: Webmasters
Beau Beckley, Patrick Wall Nick Jacobovitz – Production Asscociates
Special thanks – Satellite services provided by Siemens, Intelsat, PanAmSat and Lorel

DATA
Political advisors and support to Live 8

Make poverty history
Sarah McDougall – Assistant to Richard Curtis
Clare Bennett – Assistant to Richard Curtis
Natalie Milton – Assistant to Emma Freud
Kim Chappel – Producer Live 8 films
Zoe Edwards – Production Manager Live 8 films
Nick Fletcher – Director Live 8 films
Shonadh French – Co ordinator Live 8 international
Kate Garvey – Associate producer Long Walk
Jamie Curtis – Associate producer Live 8 new media
Amanda Horton-Mastin – Ticketing/Website
Martin Gill – Ticketing/Websight
Nicky Wimble – Press
Jackie Ball – Film maker

Ignition
Mark "Dill" Driscoll – Worldwide Director
Susan Driscoll – Worldwide Director
Bill Fitzgerald – U.S Sponsorship Management
Chris Bowers – U.S Sponsorship Management
Raymond 'O' Hora – Europe Sponsorship Management
Fred Porro – Europe Sponsorship Management
Paul Saville – Europe Sponsorship Management
Joanne Bowstead – Europe Sponsorship Management

Our sponsors:

America online
Jonathon Miller – Executive Producer

AOL US
Jim Bankoff – Senior Producer, U.S
Alix Cottrell – U.S producer
Al Reitz – Technical Director
Mari Katsunuma – Online Producer
Mimi Kim – Business Affairs

AOL Europe
Philip Rowley – Senior Producer, Europe
Betsy Scolnik – European Producer
David Shackley – Creative Director, Europe
Maryann Melchior – Project Manager
Sarah Western – Associate Producer
Caren Park – Online Production

NOKIA
Annie Laurinantti – Sponsorship Manager
Ruhne Fiala – Sponsorship Manager
Ralph Simon – Senior Strategic Advisor – Mobile

With special thanks to:

O2
Paul Samuels – Sponsorship Manager

Mobile interactive group
Nick Aldridge – Product Director
Anthony Nelson – Business Development Director
David Salgado – Chief Architect
Nick Walker – General Manager of Trinity Street

Special thanks to
Capital Radio – Prince's Trust

A major, major thanks to Ewan Hunter, Tom Hunter and Chris Gorman

With thanks to
Wesminster Council – **Tim Owen**
Metropolitan Police –
Tony Wright & Andrew Sharp
Royal Parks – **Steve Edwards & Adam Farrar**
R.A.F Northolt
Transport for London

The Peters Fraser and Dunlop group Ltd
Simon Trewin – Live 8 Literary Agent and Executive Producer
Claire Gill – Executive Producer
Maria Dawson – Legal services
Craig Dickson - Legal services
With huge thanks to **Catherine Carnie, Marc and Rob** at Getty Images, **Brian Arris, Dave Hogan, Kevin Westenberg, Tom Stoddard,** Wireimage.com, **Bernard, Kate, Neil, Maria** and all at LD Publicity Ltd, **Clare Bennett and Richard Curtis, John Kennedy, Richard Bray, Liz** at Freuds, **Paul Gorman, Gorgeous, Guy Hughes, Hannah Black and David** at Two Associates.

Paul Gorman
Alan Edwards and Julian Stockton, Outside Organisation
Bernard Doherty and his team at LD Communications
Selina Webb, Shiarra Juthan, Matt Wheeler Universal
Carole Beirne, DEP

International
Amanda Freeman, Sainted PR
Ritu Morton, 607 Press.

Scotland
Organisers:
Ewan Hunter
Chris Gorman OBE
Executive Producers:
Midge Ure OBE
Kevin Cahill
Richard Curtis
Show Director:
Lee Lodge
Advisory Director:
Tim Supple
Musical Director:
Guy Chambers
Set Design:
Jonathan Park
Producers:
Ian Coburn
Graham Pullen
Paul Roberts
Production Manager:
Chris Vaughan
Lighting Design:
Pete Barnes
Head of Artists:
Carole Winter

Media Relations:
Ewan Hunter
Jo Phillips
Elaine Webster
Kate Garvey
Scotland Event/Promoter:
DF Concerts
Unique
Chief Accountant:
Ernst & Young
Legal Consultant:
Mcgrigors solicitors
Media Partners:
BBC Scotland
Scottish Radio Holdings
Special thanks to:
Jack Maconnell & The Scottish Executive, **Lothian** & Borders Police, Edinburgh City Council, The Lord Provost Of Edinburgh, **Sir Tom Hunter, Willie Haughey, Chris Gorman Obe,** Quintessentially, Scottish Rugby Union, Virgin Airways, Virgin Rail, Stagecoach, Eurostar, Air Berlin, Data, Ticketmaster & Mig. Derek Bearhop, **Jo Phillips, Kate Garvey, Elaine Webster, Amanda Clow, Kylie Forrest, Mike Thomas, Maureen Anderson, Mary Gorman, David Kaye, Andy Rowe, Gordon & Marion White** And Many More Who Gave Willingly

Germany
German Promoter: **Marek Lieberberg, Marek Lieberberg Konzertagentur, Claudia Schulte. Marek**

Lieberberg Konzertagentur
Local Berlin Organisers: **Dieter Semelmann, Semmel Concerts, Sabine Woeste, Semmel Concerts**
Event Coordinator: **Jacky Jedlicki, Marek Lieberberg Konzertagentur**
Technical Production: **Klaus Kunzendorf, Marek Lieberberg Konzertagentur**
Radio, TV & Artist Coordinator: **Robert Fulop, Marek Lieberberg Konzertagentur, Looloo Murphy Marek Lieberberg Konzertagentur**
Press Officer **Katharina Wenisch, Marek Lieberberg Konzertagentur**
Sponsor Coordinator: **Oliver Agarwal, Marek Lieberberg Konzertagentur**
Lawyers: **Dirk Boettcher and Matthias Atrott**

Broadcasters:
Television: RBB, **Gernot Binkle, Torsten Klein**
Radio: **Peter Radszuhn**

France
Producer – **Jackie Lombard** – Inter Concerts
Production Manager –
Craig Duffy
Production Manager –
Alain Sebaoun
Production Assistant –
Bernard Lengagne
Site Facilities Manager –
Jean-Pierre Chapus
Versailles Coordinator –
Arnaud de la Villesbrunne
Castle Administrator –
Christoph Tardieu
Artist Liaison – **Magali Mohr**
TV Production – W9
Assistant to Jackie Lombard –
Cathy Sebaoun
Sound Company – On Off
Lighting Director –
Jacques Roveyrolis
Lighting Company – Regie Lumiere
Backline – Hocco, Pro-Backline and Euroconcerts
Catering – Lavina
Staging – Stage Co France & NTS
Barriers – Mojo
Riggers,Stage Crew & Runners – Tour Company
Revolving Stage – Stage One
Video Screens – I.V.S.
Power & Distribution - Magnum
Security – S.G.P.S.
Tentage/Dressing rooms - Hexa
Furniture & Ambiance - Catillon
Set Structure – Steel Monkey
Stage Banners & Scrims - Impact
Passes - Publicity & Display
SMS – WM Evenement
Public Relations – **Axele**

Schmitt
Sponsors : Montblanc
With Thanks to NRJ Radio
Team, M6 TV, **Gerard
Pullincino**
Special Thanks to – **Jack
Lang, Étienne Pinte**, the
Mayor of Versailles, **Marc
Ceronne** for sharing Versailles
with us and the Hyatt Hotel
And Thanks to Philarmonie der
Nationen, Bocelli with the
Philarmonie

Tokyo
Concert Organiser – Lily
Sobhani – BOTTLE
Japanese Production,
Sponsorship and Media:
DENTSU Casting &
Entertainment Inc: **Mr Takaaki
Ohashi, Ms Toni Pedicine,
Aki Nakajima
Tetsuhide Morooka**
Production Office Assistant –
Sakura Okamoto
Concert production:
Chief Production Manager –
Hioki Yamamura
LIFE
Disk Garage
Creativeman
Japan Press Office: **Masazumi
Komiya, Kazumi Noda & Mr
Morisaki**
UK Press Office: **Nicky
Wimble and Sophie King** –
Comic Relief
OXFAM GB Support
Claire Lewis – for being
amazing
Owain James
FUJI TV
TOKYO FM
Very Special thanks to:
Kei Mima – KANKO – For
Special support and facilities
**Mikiko Kawauchi
Atsushi Okabe** – Euclid
Agency Inc
**Emma Freud & Richard
Curtis
Lorna Dickinson
Kevin Wall**
Hottokenai

Canada
Presenters: **Dan Aykroyd &
Tom Green**
Executive Producer:
Michael Cohl
Producer: **Stephen Howard**
Consultants: **Denise Donlon &
Peter Soumalias**
House Of Blues Concerts:
**Riley O'Connor
Don Simpson
Ken Brault
Paul Corcoran
Ryan Howes
Sonja Mennie
Denise Ross
Libby Biason
Scott Phillips**

Television Broadcaster:
CTV –
**Ivan Fecan
Susanne Boyce
Ed Robinson
Mark McInnis**
Radio Broadcaster:
Sound Source Networks –
**Jean-Marie Heimrath &
Leslie Soldat**
Media Directors:
Holmes Communications –
**Kathryn Holmes & Maureen
McTague**
Venue – Park Place:
Centercorp Management –
**Terry Coughlin & Steve
Bishop**
Stage Manager: **Scott Gross**
Lighting: P.R.G. Lighting
Toronto – **Scott Gross**
Staging: Optex Staging – **Dale
Martin**
Sound: Jason Audio – **Jon
Erickson**
Audio Services: The Audio
Truck & Le Studio Mobile
Recording Engineers: **Doug
McClement & Simon Bowers**
Recording Assistants: **Danny
Greenpsoon, Peter Hamilton,
Phil Hay & Jeremy Darby**
Production Assistance: **John
Borodenko, Scott
Carmichael, Ken Craig
Allan Eistrat, Lindsay Ewing,
Howie Gold, Andrea Grant,
Dennis Griffin, Susan
Hendrickson, Sonja Mennie
& Judi MacDonald**
Artist & Music Clearances:
Eric Rosen
Catering: Wildwood Hospitality
– **John O'Brien**
Pusateri's Fine Food &
Catering – **Rob Velenik**
Security: North West Security –
Mike Doherty
Merchandise: **Anthill –
Norman Perry, Cathy
Cleghorn & Larry Warner**
Finale Producer: **Bob Ezrin**
Special Thanks To:
Gerry Barr, Canadian Council
For International Cooperation
And Make Poverty History /
Jim Rawn, World Vision
Canada / **Katia Gianneschi,**
Make Poverty History / Rogers
Wireless / WestJet /
Ticketmaster Canada /
Pusateri's / Molson Breweries /
Patron Tequila / Panasonic /
The Mod Club / Marlin Printing
& SOCAN
Live 8 Canada Is Produced by
TGA Entertainment in
Cooperation With
House of Blues Concerts

Russia
Concert Production – **Nadya
Solovieva**/Sav Entertainment
Concert shooting and
transmission – **Yuri**

Aksyuta/Figaro
Productions/Channel One
Russian Tv
TV transmission Ilya
Bachurin/Mtv Russia
General Coordination
Artemy Troitsky

Italy
Organisation Einstein
Multimedia Group
Executive producer: **Andrea
Olcese**
Organiser : **Luca Josi**
Artistic Director : **Stefano
Senardi**
Media Relations and Event
Coordinator: **Roberta Mirra**
New Media and Mobile
Relations Manager : **Anna
Maria Aloe**
Commercial & Sponsor
Relations Manager :
Gioacchino Russo
Production Managers:
**Emanuele Cadeddu, Edoardo
Geppini, Michele Olcese**
TV-director: **Stefano Mignucci**
Writer : **Giovanni Brasca**
Staff: **Francesco Biondo,
Elena Brugola, Fiorenza
Mancuso, James Milner,
Francesca Salvi, Ilaria
Spagnuolo**
Legal advisor: **Laura Miccoli**
Press Office: **Dalia Gaberscic**
: Goigest
Promoters : **Roberto de Luca**
: Clear Channel Entertainment
Italia
Ferdinando Salzano Friends &
Partners, **Claudio Trotta** :
Barley Arts
Production : Giancarlo
Campora Limelite
Media partners: RAI3, Sky,
Radio Dimensione Suono , 3
Special Thanks to the Major
Walter Veltroni and the City of
Rome, the Sponsors, the
Media, SIAE and Assomusica

Philadelphia
Kevin Wall – Executive
Producer
Tim Sexton – Executive
Producer
**Greg Sills, Ken Ehrlich, Larry
Magid**: Producers
Bruce Gowers – Director
Tisha Fein – Talent Producer
Mike Sexton, Gary Lanvy –
Coordinating Producers
Michael Ahern – Associate
Producer
**Bobby Shriver, Russell
Simmons** – Producer's
Advisory Board
Greenberg, Traurig LLPUS –
Legal Services
Phil Sama, PS – Accounting
Business Management, LLC
Chris Bowers – U.S
Sponsorship Activation
Michal Mayouhas – Assistant

to Kevin Wall
Debbie Weisberg – Assistant
to Tim Sexon
Shelly Lazar – Credentials
Beau Beckley, Patrick Wall –
Production Assistants
**Jonah Reynolds, Laurice
Rothenberg** – Webmasters
Liz Heller – Strategic Advisor
Jim Maroney – Executive in
Charge of Production

Johannesburg
The Johannesburg show was
produced in partnership with
the Global Call to Action
Against Poverty (GCAP), the
South African NGO Coalition
(SANGOCO), and CIVICUS:
World Alliance for Citizen
Participation. Additional
sponsorship support was
generously provided by Oxfam
GB, ActionAid International,
and The DCD Group. Extra
special thanks to **Kumi
Naidoo, Melanie Anstey &
John Treat** at CIVICUS.

Production Management:
**Gareth Simpson, Brad
Holmes, Paige Holmes,
Kevin Stuart, Mabusha
Masekela, Eugene Leeuw,
Themba Maseko**

Artists Booking & Love: **Antos
Stella, Charlene Foster,
Caroline Hillary**

Performers: 4 Peace
Ensemble, **Lindiwe, Mahotella
Queens, Zola, Lucky Dube,
Orchestre Baobab, Jabu
Khanyile, Oumou Sangare,
Vusi Mahlasela & Malaika.**
VJs: **Lee & Letoyah**

Guests of Honour: **Nelson
Mandela & Graca Machel**

Official Photographer:
Oscar Gutierrez

Thanks to all at CIVICUS,
Oxfam, ActionAid, SANGOCO,
the Nelson Mandela
Foundation, COSATU,
Johannesburg Development
Agency, Bassline, Gearhouse,
AS Productions, Devereux
Harris Associates, Rosin
Wright Rosengarten, South
African Police Services,
Johannesburg Metropolitan
Police Department,
Johannesburg Road Agency,
GGI Communications,
Maverick Marketing, EMS,
PPU, JHB Water, Tracker
Security & SABC.

Special thanks to **Elsabe
Booyens, Xoliswa Ngema,
Jodie Dalmeda, Owain**

James, Claire Lewis, Hassen Lorgat, Zanele Twala, Ramesh Singh, Deborah Tompkins, Zwelinzima Vavi, Mark Rosin, Greg Hamburger, Tendayi Gwata, Daryn-Lee Gamsy, Annie Williamson, Gorksie Madeira, Director Botha, Superintendent Khubeka, Captain Duvenhage, Peter Otto, Inspector Van Breda, Captain McCLoud & Team, Steve Lepita, Henri Valot, Thokozile Budaza, Philippe Roche, Bill Lawford, John Mc Dermott, Stuart Andrews, Lynn Chasan, Siphiwe Nkosi, Chris Torline, Steve Wariner, Shaun Pearce, Steve Devereux-Harris, Pam Devereux-Harris, Nicky Lawrence, Celestine Mouton, Mangoba Mkhize, Joseph Dube, Emmanuel Nalianya Kisiangani, John Samuels, David, Hannah & Miles.

Africa Calling at the Eden Project, Cornwall, UK Produced by the Eden Project in Association with WOMAD

Event concept:
Peter Gabriel, Thomas Brooman, Youssou N'Dour, Tim Smit and **Midge Ure**

At WOMAD/Realworld:
Artistic consultants: **Peter Gabriel and Youssou N'Dour**
Operations Director:
Mike Large
Artistic Director:
Thomas Brooman
Artistic Co-Director:
Annie Menter
Artistic Co-Director and Event Manager: **Paula Henderson**
Production Manager:
David Stallbaumer
Event Administrator: **Geraldine Roul**
Commercial Director:
Claire Wrightson
Stage Production Manager:
Stevie Field
Assistant to Artistic Director:
Janine Kelly
Artist hospitality management:
Jane Martinez
Press Coordinator: **Elly Butcher**
Press Coordinator: **Lucie Pemberton**
Communications Director:
Mandy Craine
Assistant to Peter Gabriel:
Annie Parsons
Assistant to Peter Gabriel & Artist Coordination:
Leanne Penfold
Artist rights and clearances:
Rob Bozas
Production Assistant:
Beckie Parsons

Production Assistant:
Sarah Lynott
Production Runner:
Willow Findlay
Recording Engineer, Open Air Stage: **Stuart Bruce**
Unit Manager, Open Air Stage: **Zoe Fawcett-Eustace**
Main Stage Audio Engineer, Open Air Stage: **Will Shapland**
Assistant Engineer, Open Air Stage: **Chris Goddard**
Assistant Engineer, Open Air Stage: **Dave Lowdoun**
Recording Engineer: Biome Stage: **Richard Chappell**
Recording Engineer Biome Stage: **Ben Findlay**
Recording Technician Biome Stage: **Dominic Monks**
Recording Technician Biome Stage: **Claire Lewis**
Lawyers: **Michael Thomas and Lance Phillips** at Sheridans
At the Eden Project
Tim Smit, Chief Executive
Howard Jones, Project Leader
David Rowe, Head of Press & PR
Chris Hines, Logistics
Jo Gale, Project Co-ordinator
Jane Montague, Production Manager
George Elworthy, General Manager
Peter Hampel, Creative Director
Mark Hole, Technical Assistance
Michael Ellis, Accountant
Linda McDonald, Sponsorship and Fundraising
Dave Meneer, Marketing Director
Emma Mansfield, Site Animation
Bryher Scudamore, Director of Communications
Jess Ratty, Communications Assistant
Ben Foster, Communications Assistant
Executive DVD Producer, Warner: **Ray Still**
DVD produced for Africa Calling by Done & Dusted
Director: **Hamish Hamilton**
Exec Producer: **Ian Stewart**
All at Done & Dusted Media
Deborah Clarke, John Casey, Kim Brown, Deborah Clarke Associates
Sarah Ransone, Producer South West, Radio 5 Live and Network Radio
Tony Sealy, BBC Radio 1 Newsbeat
Tessa Watt, Senior Producer, BBC Radio & Music Interactive
Roger Short Senior Producer, Radio 3
Shaheera Asante, Presenter, Radio 3
Virginia Crompton, Project

Leader, BBC World Class
Sarah Hellyer, David George, Simon McLennan, Alex Bodman, Louise Walter, BBC South West
Gareth Allen, ITV Westcountry
Photographers
Sophia Milligan, Steve Tanner, Charles Francis, David Hastilow, Apex, Theo Moye
Production Crew
Ade Burt, Technical Manager
Allan Drake, Crew Chief
Food for Films
Harlequin Flooring
Fearless Audio
Hall for Cornwall
Hardware for Xenon Projection
AMP Plant Hire
GE Energy Generators
LightMedia for LED Screens
S + H Drapes
Sean Donohoe, Set Design
Technical Assistance
Dave Rogers, Julie Garden, Cisco Systems, **Peter Hollands**, Consultant; **Ben Verwaayen, James Adcock, Jeremy Hallsworth, Darren Parker, Dave Kumar, David Hawkins, Peter Coles, Mathew Sullivan,** BT
Stage Managers: Open Air Stage, **Stevie Field.** Biome Stage, **Tony Morris and Jack Morrison**
Lighting systems supplied by Neg Earth
Lighting Designer: **Tellson James**
Crew Chief: **Ben Morgan**
Spotlights: **John Dall**
Lampy: **Alex Melville**
Technician: **Paul Sadler**
Versatiles: **Rob Fowler**
Office: **Dave Ridgeway**
Audio system by AMPCO Pro Rent
Audio Production Manager and Front of House: **Dieter van Denzel**
System and Front of House: **Jeroen Ebskamp**
Monitor: **Steve Watson**
Monitor and Stage: **Koen Benschop**
Stage and Backline: **John(Cable) Hessing**
Driver: **Peter P. de Haas**
StageTruck: **Peter Beresford** and **Jason McGurk**
Drivers: **Nick Dashwood and Simon Evans**
Artist welfare: **Saimon Mambazo, Ben Menter, Phil Vandervert**
Eden Team / Eden Associates / Eden Volunteers
African Co-ordination
Kwesi Owuso, Creative Storm, Ghana
Hellen Tombo, KYCEP Johannesburg Link
Gareth Simpson, Oxfam South Africa; **John Samual,**

Mandela Foundation; **Lord Joel Joffe; Melanie Anstey; Hassen Lorgat; Kumi Naidoo**
Special Thanks to:
Western Morning News; Cornwall Fire Brigade; Devon & Cornwall Constabulary
Sue Leath, Jade Rowse, Carol Lock, Restormel Licensing; Richard Thompson, Nigel Winn, Restormel Building Control; **Simon Hall, Eric Coon,** Restormel Environmental Health; **Sq Ldr David Webster, RAF St Mawgan; Alistair Spencer,** Joint Maritime Facility, St Mawgan; **Doreen George,** RNAS Culdrose; Mathew Taylor MP; **Angus Watt** and team; The World Famous Firework Co; Hewaswater Scaffolding; Coast 2 Coast Security; STOUT Security
All our fantastic Sponsors

and to everybody else worldwide who made Live8 possible.

This book was written, designed, typeset and made ready for printing in 11 days. **The Random House Group** would like to thank all those who made this possible including: **Brian Aris, Paul Ashton, Neil Bradford, Rhidian Brook, Phil Dent, Bernard Doherty, David Eldridge, James Empringham, Robert Hackett, Dominic Cooper, Kevan Westbury, Yoko Yamaguchi** and **Angelo Acanfora** at Two Associates, **Bob Geldof,** Getty Images, **Claire Gill, Harvey Goldsmith, Paul Gorman, Dave Hogan, John Kennedy, Tom Stoddart, Simon Trewin, Paul Vallely, Kevin Westenberg,** Wireimages.com and all at Live 8.

The printing and binding of this book took 7 days. Special thanks to the **APPL Group**, Wemding, Germany (www.appl.de). Bound by Oldenbourg Buchmanufaktur, Monheim, Germany (www.oldenbourg.com). Laminated by Achilles Group, Celle, Germany (www.achilles.de). Printed by Appl Druck, Wemding, Germany on LuxoArt Silk, 135gsm. Produced by M-real Biberist, Switzerland, distributed by Schneidersöhne,Ulm,Germany (www.schneidersoehne.de).

Photo credits

Brian Aris/Getty Images, **Paul Ashton**/Getty Images, **Alessandro Benedetti**/Wireimage.com, **Dave Benett**/Getty Images **Daniel Berehulak**/Getty Images, **Eric Bouvet**/Getty Images, **William Thomas Cain**/Getty Images, **Matt Cardy**/Getty Images, **Phil Dent, George Chin**/Wireimage.com, **David Fisher**, **Henner Frankenfeld**/Getty Images, **Sean Gallup**/Getty Images, **Jo Hale**/Getty Images, **Dave Hogan, Chris Jackson**/Getty Images, **Koichi Kamoshida**/Getty Images, **MJ Kim**/Getty Images, **Junko Kimura**/Getty Images, **Oleg Nikishin**/Getty Images, **Yuji Ohsugi**/Wireimage.com, **Franco Origlia**/Getty Images, **Steve Reigate, Andreas Rentz**/Getty Images, **Fyodor Savintsev**/Wireimage.com, **Pascal Le Segretain**/Getty Images, **Kurt Vinion**/Wireimage.com, **Paul Webb, Donald Weber**/Getty Images, **Kevin Westenberg**/Getty Images, **George Widman-Pool**/Getty Images